33⅓

MARQUEE MO

Praise for the series:

It was only a matter of time before a clever publisher realized that there is an audience for whom *Exile on Main Street* or *Electric Ladyland* are as significant and worthy of study as *The Catcher in the Rye* or *Middlemarch* ... The series ... is freewheeling and eclectic, ranging from minute rock-geek analysis to idiosyncratic personal celebration — *The New York Times Book Review*

Ideal for the rock geek who thinks liner notes just aren't enough — *Rolling Stone*

One of the coolest publishing imprints on the planet — *Bookslut*

These are for the insane collectors out there who appreciate fantastic design, well-executed thinking, and things that make your house look cool. Each volume in this series takes a seminal album and breaks it down in startling minutiae. We love these. We are huge nerds — *Vice*

A brilliant series ... each one a work of real love — *NME* (UK)

Passionate, obsessive, and smart — *Nylon*

Religious tracts for the rock 'n' roll faithful — *Boldtype*

[A] consistently excellent series — *Uncut* (UK)

We ... aren't naïve enough to think that we're your only source for reading about music (but if we had our way ... watch out). For those of you who really like to know everything there is to know about an album, you'd do well to check out Continuum's "33 1/3" series of books — *Pitchfork*

For reviews of individual titles in the series, please visit our blog at 333sound.com and our website at http://www.bloomsbury.com/musicandsoundstudies

Follow us on Twitter: @333books

Like us on Facebook: https://www.facebook.com/33.3books

For a complete list of books in this series, see the back of this book

33⅓

For more information about the series, please visit our new blog:

www.333sound.com

Where you'll find:

– Author and artist interviews

– Author profiles

– News about the series

– How to submit a proposal to our open call

– Things we find amusing

Marquee Moon

Bryan Waterman

BLOOMSBURY ACADEMIC
NEW YORK • LONDON • OXFORD • NEW DELHI • SYDNEY

BLOOMSBURY ACADEMIC
Bloomsbury Publishing Inc
1385 Broadway, New York, NY 10018, USA

BLOOMSBURY, BLOOMSBURY ACADEMIC and the Diana logo
are trademarks of Bloomsbury Publishing Plc

First published in 2011 by the Continuum International Publishing Group Inc
Reprinted by Bloomsbury Academic 2013, 2014, 2016, 2017, 2018 (twice), 2020

A catalog record for this book is available from the Library of Congress.

ISBN: PB: 978-1-4411-8605-8
ePDF: 978-1-4411-4529-1
eBook: 978-1-4411-2777-8

Series: 33 1/3, volume 83

Typeset by Pindar
Printed and bound in the United States of America

To find out more about our authors and books visit www.bloomsbury.com
and sign up for our newsletters.

for Sacha, Derick, and Linda
and with gratitude to Stephanie

On their bitter guitars
These libertines strike the shrill string;
Intoning the chants bizarre,
Nostalgic and revolting.

— Paul Verlaine, from "Grotesques" (1866)

Contents

Acknowledgments

Thanks above all to Stephanie Smith-Waterman, whose patience, love, and support made this book — and make anything else I do — possible. Thanks also to Anna, Molly, and Charlie for going without a dad far too often in the last six months. I'm grateful to David Barker for taking on the project and waiting patiently for the results, and to Cyrus Patell, partner in New York literary crimes, for reactions to multiple drafts. Sean Nortz provided invaluable research/library assistance, especially at the very beginning and the very end. The librarians at Fales Library and Special Collections at NYU deserve many thanks, especially Marvin Taylor, who has assembled the world's premier collection of materials related to New York's Downtown Scene, 1974–1984. Thanks also to Lisa Darms, Senior Archivist at Fales, for timely help with images, and to Bobst Library's Interlibrary Loan staff. I am indebted to two Television fans I've never met: Keith Allison, for his Television website The Wonder, which collects a large number of articles about the band, some of which I wasn't able to track down elsewhere; and Phil Obbard, for maintaining the Marquee Moon Mailing List, whose archived discussions cover every conceivable aspect of the band and this album. My friend Jason Connolly first gave me the itch to write for this series. Jason Gross of the online magazine Perfect Sound Forever helped me track down the photo of Richard Lloyd in the famous Please Kill Me T-Shirt. Special thanks to Michael Carlucci, Richard Hell, and Andy Schwartz for permission to reproduce the images I wanted. All material from the Richard Hell Papers is quoted by permission. I have been carried along, whether or not they knew it, by friends in the downtown NYC blogosphere — Tim Broun of Stupefaction, EV Grieve, and Alex Smith of Flaming Pablum. Bryan Kuntz (aka NYCDreamin) of the blog This Ain't the Summer of Love helped me in attempts to track down arcane bits of info. My brother, Nathan, helped me scour the Web for bootlegs I didn't already own. Jim Rader, author of my favorite piece on early Television, has been a generous correspondent. I've also benefited from conversations with Daniel Kane, whose work on the LES's interstitial scenes is inspirational. My students in Writing New York and Downtown Scenes helped me think through several ideas that made their way here, as did friends at The Great Whatsit. Special thanks for many conversations about music to Sacha Jones, Derick Melander, and Linda Perkins, my fellow members of the original Record Club New York.

Prelude

> Obviously what was going on here was the earliest germinal stage of the late-Seventies American punk rock scene, which eventually exploded in three places: New York, London, and the international communications media.
>
> — *Lester Bangs, on the early CBGB's scene,*
> *in* Blondie *(1980)*

The first album I ever paid for with my own money was an LP born in the waning days — some would say the death throes — of CBGB's first generation: Blondie's *Parallel Lines*, released in the fall of 1978, a few months after Television's sophomore album, *Adventure*. I would have been eight or nine years old. I lived in a rural, cedar-ringed town in the mountains of northern Arizona, and would not have heard of Blondie for several more years if it hadn't been for my uncle, living in the metropolitan Phoenix area, who received the record in the mail as part of an LP club and, as a devout listener of George Thorogood and Ted Nugent, had no interest in Debbie Harry and her black-and-white-striped mod squad. To me, though, the cover seemed stunning, otherworldy, and I gladly forked over his asking price of 25 cents. In retrospect I'd like to think it was a defining moment in my musical development, the moment I could no longer abide my parents' Carpenters and Bee Gees and Neil Sedaka records that had defined my Seventies (which is to say, my life) to that point. Maybe it was. My clearer memory, though, is that my father, who also had records by the Rascals and the Stones, thought my 5th grade teacher, his best friend and an avowed Abba fan, would dig Blondie's girl-group vocals, and so I took the record to school for show and tell. We played it one afternoon in class as a reward for good behavior, though Mr. Smith, who'd previewed the lyrics sheet, made me stand like a sentinel by the turntable and jerk down the volume each time the word "ass" appeared in the song "Heart of Glass." Maybe that record didn't change my life, though I did wear it out. And somewhere in my parents' library is a cassette tape of me singing my prepubescent heart out to that nuclear holocaust deep cut, "Fade Away and Radiate."

I start with this anecdote not simply to situate myself chronologically or geographically in relation to the downtown New York scene this book seeks to reconstruct — and not merely to warn readers up front that I wasn't at CBGB's in the '70s along with the dog shit, the bums, and the birth of the music that would define the rest of my life (to this point) — but to note that it had taken only four years for a dirty index finger of a bar on the Bowery in New York, a city of which I had almost no conception outside *Sesame Street*, to escape its underground origins and erupt into mainstream American consciousness, reaching even the rural hinterlands — all without the help of the internet. If you'd told someone at CBGB's in the spring of '74 that four years later the brassy blonde singer for the Stillettoes [*sic*] would have a record that sold 20 million copies, they would have assumed you'd been smoking up behind the club between sets. And yet here she was, arriving unsolicited in my uncle's post office box, simply because he forgot to return a slip telling Columbia House he didn't want his record of the month.

Not that I would know anything about CBGB's or the Bowery for several years to come. That knowledge I pieced together as a teenager via a subscriptions to mainstream rock magazines and my discovery of the *Readers' Guide to Periodicals* and Interlibrary Loan. Sending off for photocopies of old articles on my favorite bands, I learned that the post-punk/new wave music that filled my teenage years — thanks to hip kids I met at orchestra camp in the summers, and also to John Peel, whose show played very late nights on a KTNN, the Navajo Nation's radio station — traced its genealogy back directly to that same club's earliest bands: Television, Blondie, the Ramones, Patti Smith, Talking Heads. Even so, when I first read about REM's admiring Television or U2's declaration of indebtedness to the whole CBGB's scene, I still knew no one who had even a third-generation dubbed cassette tape of Television's or Patti Smith's albums. My music, like my uncle's before me, came primarily by mail-order, and I don't recall CBGB's old-timers as part of the catalog, with the exception of Talking Heads and Blondie, who'd scored a handful of pop hits in the '80s. That very distinction — the commercial success of a few of the groups and the total unavailability of others — rendered Television or Patti Smith all the more iconic.

It wasn't until later — when I was a college student, then a graduate student in American Studies, situated in more suitable climes in east coast urban centers — that the full CBGB's constellation came into view. In college, outside the confines of pre-internet Smallville, I found friends with similar tastes and crates full of records I'd heard of but never seen, all mine for the cost of a few dozen blank cassettes. Serious record stores became a reality, not something I read about. Just about the time I finished my PhD, Napster (then Audiogalaxy, then Soulseek) became available and then even the most elusive bootlegs could be mine with a few keystrokes. Rather than spend much time on the music I had grown up with in the '80s, I found myself repeatedly drawn to the sounds and music mythology of earlier eras. The bands that dominated my music listening in the '90s — the whole American Pixies-and-Pavement-inspired indie scene — were name-checking Television the same way my post-punk idols had.

In spite of the fact that CBGB's logo has become as ubiquitous as Journey songs at a wedding dance, the club's location at 315 Bowery given over to high-end retailers who want to cash in on rock chic and four decades of neighborhood hipness, Television remains not just a cult band but a cool kids' cult band. Television still separates sheep from goats, righteous rock snobs from Philistines. I don't remember the first time I listened to *Marquee Moon*, but I do remember my first conversations about Television, with my friend Shelley in her Brooklyn apartment, before I moved to New York. Shelley oozes cool, cuts through crap with razor-sharp observations and, as anyone who's ever received a mix-tape from her knows, can work a 90-minute freeform mix like few others. Shelley called me out once long ago for not having taken *Adventure* seriously enough. She was right: Wanna hear where American college rock came from? Listen to "Days." It will make you question your early devotion to REM. And *Adventure* was supposed to be a sophomore slump.

If Television's story in the '70s was a continual effort to break out of the New York scene it helped to found, the fact that its records remained underground following its four-year flirtation with fame meant that it would always be the province of in-groups, those who transmitted secret knowledge from one rock underground to another via record-store recommendations, fanzines, mix-tapes, college radio shows, and podcasts, all transmitted with a kind of Masonic solemnity. Television lends itself to the genre of secret history: its members were mythologizing the band before it was even born, which means more often than not its story gets told in fits of nostalgia for a club and a neighborhood scene and a glorious moment in rock 'n' roll that no longer exists. In aiming to present a cultural history of that scene, 1973–1978, using Television and the music on and leading up to *Marquee Moon* as windows onto that world, I aim less to recycle these myths than to ask how and why this music was produced when it was, and what purposes it served for those who created it and continue to find so much meaning in it.

Some portions of what follows will be familiar to the thousands who still fixate on this scene: the recognizable names CBGB's spawned, the infighting between Television's members, the aborted early sessions with Brian Eno, Richard Hell's acrimonious departure from the band. But my approach here is less a rock journalist's than that of a literary and cultural historian with an archival bent and an eye for details that don't quite fit the standard story. My biggest motivation in writing this book is to offer a more carefully documented reception history than you'll find in the gossipy books on the scene that, if given the chance, go for sensation over substance, let alone discussion of the music itself. I'm interested, rather, in how tradition forms and fractures, in the origins of sounds that seemed so new when Tom Verlaine started warbling for audiences, or when he and Richard Lloyd first aimed dueling guitar lines at one another like lightning striking itself.

Introduction
Origin Myths, or, Just Trying to Tell a Vision

Jest the Facts
— *Sgt. Friday, "Dragnet," and Tom Verlaine,*
"Prove It," as cited by Richard Hell, 1974

I don't think that anybody's memory is infallible.
— *Tom Verlaine, Q, 1992*

It's the closest thing New York punk — and by extension all of punk, post-punk, new wave, college, alternative, and indie rock — has to an origin myth: A couple kids in their early twenties walk south on the Bowery through New York's Lower East Side on a spring afternoon in 1974, just as the owner of a club at the intersection of Bleecker Street — a Hell's Angels dive called Hilly's — climbs a ladder to hang a new awning for his venue. He's renaming the place CBGB & OMFUG, which, he tells the passers-by, stands for Country, Bluegrass, and Blues, and Other Music for Uplifting Gormandizers. They tell him that's exactly what they play — along with a few originals — and somehow manage to get a date out of him. Of course they're lying, but for their first night they round up friends and buy enough drinks that they land a regular string of Sundays. On stage, they wear ripped T-shirts, short hair. Noisy songs, bastard children of '60s basement sounds: raw, angular, amateurish. Rough as hell. The owner thinks they're terrible, but audiences trickle in. By mid-summer more new bands turn up. Some of these will become famous. But this band, Television, was first on the scene. And CBGB — or CBGB's or CB's, to its habitués, as if it belonged to someone named CB instead of to a guy named Hilly — would become world famous as the birthplace of punk.

This origin myth, which settled quickly into a more or less permanent form, started turning up in profile pieces on Television in 1976, just as "punk" and CBGB's itself sparked mainstream media attention and just as Television was finally signing a contract for its debut album. When *Marquee Moon* was released in February 1977, fans and critics listened to it primarily in relation to what was already being called CBGB's "mythology" or its "annals," as if the club were as old and storied as the famous Marquee in London, where the Stones, the Who, the Yardbirds, and Bowie had all cut their chops. Writing in the national publication *Hit Parader* in early 1977, James Wolcott (who'd already analyzed "the rise of punk rock" in the *Village Voice*) describes yellowed CBGB's mementoes tacked to his "albino-white walls": the moment was fading, just three years in. For Wolcott, the myth was already established:

"[T]here literally would be no CBGB scene in New York if it weren't for Television," he writes. "[I]t was [Tom] Verlaine and [Richard] Lloyd who originally conned — I mean persuaded — Hilly Kristal to let a rock band play there, and TV played when the bar was nothing but dog dung, broken bottles, and reeling, vomiting winos."[1]

Appearing in almost four decades' worth of articles, popular histories, memoirs, and band biographies, this founding narrative functions as avant-garde origin stories most often do: as a "parable of absolute self creation," presenting the underground movement as self-generated, a clean break from whatever came before.[2] The narrative cuts off cultural memory and obscures influence. Even histories that trace New York punk to earlier sounds — Detroit bands like the Stooges or the MC5, New York underground acts like the Velvet Underground and the New York Dolls — still manage to portray Television and CBGB's springing, like conjoined twins, from the broken glass and needle-strewn streets of an economically depressed lower Manhattan in that second summer of Watergate.

Of course it's tempting just to print that legend and move on. Legend counts for something after all. But the closer you look at where this story comes from and how it became commonplace, minor variations become meaningful. Verlaine and Lloyd both started

---

1 Wolcott (1977).
2 Krauss (1981: p. 53).

telling the origin story just prior to *Marquee Moon*'s release, though Lloyd's renditions have been canonized in the competing sacred histories of New York punk, Clinton Heylin's *From the Velvets to the Voidoids* (1993), and Legs McNeil and Gillian McCain's *Please Kill Me* (1996), as well as in the only book-length history of CBGB's, Roman Kozak's long out-of-print *This Ain't No Disco* (1987). Lloyd's storytelling is detailed, dramatic, and chuck-full of dialogue, as if these stories have always existed in narrative form. Here he is in the mid-1980s:

> One day Tom came and he said, "I saw this fucking hick, like up on a stepladder — he's opening a bar, calling it CB or something, GB. Do you want to go up there and we'll talk the guy into letting us play?" I said, "Yeah, of course." So after rehearsal we walked up, and Hilly was outside standing on a stepladder, putting up the awning. We called him down and he came in with us, and I bought a drink and I think Tommy had one of his rare white russians. We said, "What are you calling the place? Are you going to have live music?" And he said, "Yes, I'm calling it country, bluegrass and blues and other music for 'undernourished' gourmandizers." That's what OMFUG is. Anyway, he asked, "Do you play country?" We said, "Yeah, we play country." He said, "Do you play blues and bluegrass?" We said, "We play blues, bluegrass, anything you want, we'll play it." And he said, "Alright," and penciled us in for the Sunday.[3]

---

3 Kozak (1988: p. 13).

Take a closer look at what this quote reveals. For one, it already contains clichés, as suggested by Lloyd's repetition of the stepladder detail at the start. More importantly, though, Lloyd ventriloquizes Verlaine to make Hilly seem foolish: A hick! Opening a country bar on the Bowery! By contrast, Television's members are trickster heroes, wily enough to win the gig. Success was secured when their manager, Terry Ork, bought "enough drinks by himself to set the place up. By God," Lloyd exclaims, "Hilly was making money."[4]

Compare Lloyd's account with Kristal's, from CBGB's website: "I was on a ladder in front of the club fixing the awning in place, when I looked down to notice three scruffy dudes in torn jeans and T shirts looking up at me inquisitively."[5] That would be Verlaine, Lloyd, and Richard Hell, three-fourths of the band. Hilly's inclusion of Hell makes you wonder: did Lloyd's memory lapse in the omission, or has Hell been squeezed out of the story as well as the band? In 1976, when Lloyd first put his version in print, he also gave only himself and Verlaine the credit.[6] Hilly, by contrast, downplays Television's role in favor of his own as impresario, scenemaker, gruff but loving patriarch. He'd managed the famed Village Vanguard jazz club, for God's sake. He'd opened his bar on the Bowery because artists and musicians were already flocking to cheap east side apartments and loft spaces

---

4 Kozak (1988: p. 13).
5 Kristal, "The History of CBGB & OMFUG."
6 Gholson (1976).

in nearby SoHo. Hilly's earliest versions of the story, in fact, directly refute the band's: "Television were *not* the first" on the scene, he insisted, they were just "the first to be successful. Actually, it was Terry Ork who badgered me into having Television back time and time again, because they were so god-awful when they started."[7]

In 1978, when Kristal gave this quote to London's *New Musical Express*, Verlaine had already distanced himself from the original CB's scene; Hilly's feelings seem a little sore. Then, within months of the *NME* article, Television would call it quits, having toured briefly in support of its second album, *Adventure*. And Verlaine, who'd asserted Television's claim as CBGB's founders, insisted there had never *really* been a scene at all: "Newspapers were making it into a scene," he said, "but to me it was just a club we played for three years."[8]

Marquee Moon emerged in part from Verlaine's ambivalence on this point. He wanted credit for starting a scene he feared would box him in, and as a result Television's debut both grows and departs from the downtown scene, marked by entry and exit in specific ways. A monument to the beginning and the ending of the scene's founding era, the album, like the band, has been understood from its time to our own as intimately linked to the story of a broader movement, including the story's emergence in international print, in

---

7 Murray (1978).
8 Heylin (1993: p. 321).

some cases before the music had even made it across the pond. Taking seriously Lester Bangs's comment that one of punk's birthplaces was the international media, I've chosen to write about *Marquee Moon* in that context, as emerging from a dialogue between the music and the way the band was portrayed in print.

As should already be clear, any punk origin story will inevitably betray some idea about who deserves credit for heroic acts of avant-garde self-creation. Even among the accounts told by Television's members, disparities abound. Verlaine tells one version where he's accompanied not by band mates but by a ragtime-playing buddy named Alan Ostlund.[9] Hell would claim that *he'd* been scouting out venues to replace the Mercer Arts Center, a key site on the underground until the building collapsed a few months before Hilly renamed his Bowery club.[10] Hell would also argue his status as punk founder had been robbed, both by his exit from Television in early 1975 and by the London pop svengali and haberdasher Malcolm McLaren, who blatantly ripped off his style to create the Sex Pistols.[11] This alternative account eventually morphed into a version of the origin story featuring Hell solo: "Exactly because [CBGB's] was an unprepossessing dive that stank from the piss of the winos upstairs," the London *Independent* wrote in 2008, "Hell had discovered a place where punk could germinate uncontaminated

---

9 "Tom Verlaine" (1995).
10 McNeil and McCain (1996: p. 169).
11 Hell (1980).

by outside interest."[12] And Hell's not alone in taking or getting credit for a role in the story that typically goes to Verlaine. Lloyd recently exclaimed to one interviewer: "CBGBs is the most famous rock 'n' roll club to have ever existed and I fucking created it!"[13]

These attempts to secure credit aren't limited to individuals: Joey Ramone on occasion made the specious claim that the Ramones were first on the CB's scene.[14] But the fact that so many punk heroes came from one dive bar also underscores the importance of community to the scene's start. As Blondie's Clem Burke puts it, CB's bands "were also the audience. In the beginning it was this little microcosm of hip culture that no one else knew about."[15] Hell concurs: "At CBGB's, we imagined our own world into being, because we didn't feel comfortable in the existing one. It was a place you could go to every night and feel like you belonged. And that's because it flowered out of our own brains."[16] In Kristal's *New York Times* obit in 2007, Jon Pareles promotes this communal ethos by crediting Patti Smith along with Verlaine for stumbling onto Hilly's bar while on their way to William Burroughs's "Bunker," the converted YMCA at 222 Bowery where the Beat icon lived in the 1970s. Though this account can't possibly be accurate — Smith and Verlaine

12 Hasted (2005).
13 "Endurance: The Richard Lloyd Interview" (2007).
14 Black (1985).
15 Fletcher (2009: p. 342).
16 Hasted (2005).

wouldn't meet until Television had already started playing the club — the invocation of Burroughs as the scene's spiritual godfather is something Smith has frequently cited herself, linking CB's punks to downtown predecessors, the Beats. So much for self-creation.

Marquee Moon doesn't trumpet its own origins. It seems, in fact, out of time, perpetually new, like a dispatch from rock's future. It nonetheless emerged from and plays into this desire to mark new beginnings. As Heylin argues, the Television of *Marquee Moon* was quite a different band than the one that first played CBGB's in March 1974, but he still lists *Marquee Moon* as one of American punk's four "most enduring landmarks." (The others are Patti Smith's *Horses*, Pere Ubu's *The Modern Dance*, and Richard Hell and the Voidoids' *Blank Generation*.) Moreover, he deems *Marquee Moon* "probably the most dramatic debut of any American rock band."[17] This album has, from its release, sent rock historians scrambling to situate it, in spite of the fact that its audience has never been as broad as it deserves. One of the paradoxes of Television's trajectory is that mainstream success might have prevented the band's pre-eminence in critical estimations: its cult status buttresses the album's claims on authenticity and originality.

In cementing Television's centrality to punk's origins, no text plays as significant a role as McNeil and McCain's *Please Kill Me*, in spite of the fact that, compared to Heylin's history, it devotes more attention to sex and drugs than to the revolutionary

17 Heylin (1993: pp. 351, 275).

music. *Please Kill Me*, which takes its very title from a legendary T-shirt Hell designed and Lloyd wore on stage, offers a wistful glance at a gritty pre-AIDS '70s New York rock scene. It has two clear agendas where Television's concerned: First, it argues that Television laid foundations for American punk well before the Sex Pistols were a glint in McLaren's eye. Second, it makes Hell the scene's unsung hero. Hell's heroism is defined not simply against McLaren's thievery, but also against Verlaine's desire for complete control of Television, which resulted in Hell's departure.

The early/late Television split is almost as important to the band's mythology as the discovery of the club. Decades later you'll find partisans still facing off. If they preferred Television with Hell, they would rather hear early bootlegs and rougher arrangements than the finished versions on *Marquee Moon*. To them, the album might as well have come from a different band. Others will tell you that Television only benefitted from Fred Smith's more subtle and supple bass. If *Marquee Moon*'s story can't be told without covering the Hell/Verlaine fallout, this should only remind us that creation myths also serve to explain the emergence of good and evil, gods and devils, heroes and villains. They outline rituals for preserving the purity of such categories and reinforcing tribal identity. In *Please Kill Me*, Verlaine and his consort Patti Smith come off as devils in disguise.

And then there are the alternate accounts that make Television *and* Legs McNeil the villains while valorizing New York's earlier glitter scene as punk's true fountainhead. The notion that CBGB's founding marked glitter's grave still gets a rise out of those who emphasize the continuity between the Mercer Arts Center and the later scene. This camp complains that back when CB's was still Hilly's on the Bowery, the club's acts included glitter pioneers Eric Emerson and the Magic Tramps and the transgendered drag artist Wayne (later Jayne) County, whose backing bands included Queen Elizabeth, the Electric Chairs, and the Backstreet Boys. "Queen Elizabeth actually played CBGB's four months before Television," Jayne County complained in 2005. "I love Television, but enough of this shit, give Jayne credit!"[18] Fair enough. If we want to understand the mythology that consolidated around Television, perhaps we'll have to ask not just what that story's longevity means, but also what other possible pasts the myth obscures, and how those historical alternatives might relate to the music that eventually became *Marquee Moon*.

CBGB's significance in our own day derives from a desire to preserve the authenticity of New York's East side neighborhoods, long a stand-in for the possibility of artistic subculture itself, or perhaps for the spark of authentic rebellion at the heart of rock 'n' roll. (Consider, though, that we're twice as far removed from the mid-'70s as the downtown bands were from the birth of rock 'n' roll in the '50s.) But anxieties about downtown's decline or rock's relevance bring up yet another purpose served by avant-garde origin myths: the preservation of community by excluding late arrivals. Such a posture ironically represses CBGB's own role as

---

18 Nobakht (2005: p. 73); Holmstrom (2007).

vanguard of Bowery gentrification. In the 1980s, Karen Kristal, Hilly's ex-wife, proudly rebroadcasted NYPD opinion "that CBGB has done more than anything else to clean up the area and bring safety."[19] But to others these transformations already heralded the traditional neighborhood's death: Richard Hell wasn't on the East Side because his "folks have just pulled in from Puerto Rico," wrote the critic Vivien Goldman in 1977. He's "one of the new generation of artist types flocking to low-rent areas, a process which will inevitably result in the rents slowly rising, the scabrous tenements being tarted up till the immigrant families can't afford it any more."[20] In our century, nostalgia not for displaced immigrants but for displaced bohemians has worn itself thin in the mass production of CBGB's paraphernalia. In 1976 bohemian nostalgists already told stories about a time at CBGB's before limousines delivered celebrity slummers onto the scene. Part of the bohemian legacy, of course, is mourning and memorializing an authentic past, as is recognizing the "elusiveness of authentic experience."[21] To many fans, *Marquee Moon* serves just such a function, perhaps more than ever.

The authentic past eludes us precisely because we ritually sacrifice memory to create mythical accounts of origins — and endings. When Television reunited in 1992 to record a third album, at least one bemused interviewer sat by while the band had it out over the

---

19 Kozak (1988: p. 3).

20 Goldman (1977).

21 Bradshaw (2010: p. 158).

details of their own legend. Verlaine took issue with the way Lloyd had recounted their breakup for over a decade:

> Verlaine: "Richard remembers this dinner in August 1978 where we all got together and broke up. I don't remember that. Billy doesn't remember that."
>
> Ficca: "I don't remember that."
>
> Verlaine: "Fred doesn't remember that."
>
> Smith: "I really can't remember that."
>
> Verlaine: "Richard says we went to Chinatown and ate chow mein or something."
>
> Lloyd: "No, no. Tom called me up and he said, I'm thinking of leaving the band and I said, Well, you don't have to leave the band because I'm thinking of leaving the band too, so why don't we just call it a day? And we called up Fred and Billy and we said, We'll meet at The Loft, which was in Chinatown, and we'll make it a happy event rather than a sad one. And then when we got there, Tom was the one that mentioned Moby Grape because I had Moby Grape records . . ."
>
> Verlaine: "The man's memory!"
>
> Lloyd: ". . . so we went out to this Chinese joint in an alley in Chinatown we used to call Whore Alley . . ."
>
> Verlaine (*deciding at this point to stop his pacing and lie face down in the middle of the long table*): "The guy is cracked!"
>
> Lloyd: ". . . and we had dinner and we told jokes and then we split. And then we went on our dismal way."
>
> Verlaine: "Speak for yourself!"
>
> Lloyd: "I just did. I have a very good memory . . ."
>
> . . . The tiff continues . . .

Verlaine: "I'm not dismissing what you're saying. I'm merely saying that I don't think that anybody's memory is infallible. All I'm saying is that the three of us don't remember the dinner . . ."

Lloyd: "That we all went to! That's incredible!"[22]

Memory isn't infallible. Myths settle into lives of their own. Collaboratively produced, they lay claim on originality, authorship, and agency. Television lasted, in its original run, from 1973 to 1978. CBGB's had a longer life, but still died an early death in 2006. (At 33, it was the same age as the crucified Christ, as Patti Smith noted at the time.) The club was replaced by a John Varvatos boutique that tries in its own way to preserve the rock club's feel — down to preserving original graffiti — while hocking $3500 rocker jackets. In this century, the consensus myth of CBGB's origins doesn't require a villain from within: gentrification has usurped that role. Awnings will come and go. But pilgrims will continue to worship at the intersection of Bowery and Bleecker. They'll close their eyes and imagine a different entrance at number 315. Then they'll cue up a favorite album, adjust their headphones, and wander south, toward Chinatown, tracing an earlier generation's movements through tight toy nights.

---

22 Hibbert (1992).

1
Some Big Set-Up: New York Bohemia

> The Beat thing happened when I was younger. I used to run away from home, inspired by the Beats, like in '64 and '65.
> — *Tom Verlaine*, Raygun, *November 1994*

> I was a beardless seventeen-year-old stick figure, all wrists and ankles, with rumpled hair starting to cover my ears, little wire glasses that had a thin tortoise shell casing around their round lenses, work shirt, jeans and not much sign of any status outside of dispossessed youth. I did look like a poet.
> — *Richard Hell*, Brooklyn Rail, *October 2007*

Marquee Moon is a quintessential album of the New York night. In its lower Manhattan landscape — largely desolate — darkness resounds with sirens, clangs, revving engines, the subway's rattling tracks. The album has a literary landscape, too, filled (contrary to myths of self-creation) with echoes of New York's long bohemian traditions, celebrations of freedoms found in the city's dark patches and forgotten corners. Television joins a parade of writers and artists, from Walt Whitman to Hart Crane, Marcel Duchamp to Jackson Pollack, Frank O'Hara and Allen Ginsberg to the band's contemporary, Jim Carroll, along with musicians working in jazz traditions, all of whom contribute to an artistic mode we call the urban pastoral. If ancient Greek pastorals celebrated the virtues of country life (personal freedom, repose, delight in nature, escape from social conventions), Television's debut album echoes dozens of urban predecessors in the conviction that these qualities are even more intense in cities, where they rub up against opposite extremes of degradation, claustrophobia, and the excessively unnatural.[1] *Marquee Moon*'s very title combines urban and pastoral imagery, suggesting the kind of night sky only visible above the neon glare of city-dwellers' assault on the dark. By implication the marquee, not the actual moon, sets the album's mood.

The album's title also suggests that sensory experience will be of prime importance to these eight songs. What can we see by the light of a marquee moon? What will be revealed on *Marquee Moon*'s grooves? If its songs reverberate with an urban soundscape and echo artistic forerunners, they abound with references to other senses — and sensory derangement — in general: vision and blindness; flashes of transcendental revelation; dizzying heights; the smell of a seaport. When Verlaine sings "My senses are sharp and my

---

1 Gray (2010).

hands are like gloves" he's not just suggesting that his nighttime wanderings are filtered through "some new kind of drug": he's recognizing general conditions of corporeality and consciousness. Hyperconsciousness, even: the album is full of hesitations, pauses, periods of waiting — sometimes for several minutes — while the music builds and then recedes, like a tide pulled by lunar gravity. So much time to think. If these hesitations seem nervous they also allow for delayed gratification.

From the beginning, Television's New York nocturne has frequently been compared to the Velvet Underground's a decade earlier, but Verlaine's reportage fundamentally differs from Lou Reed's. Reed is a realist. Think of the detachment with which he narrates "Heroin," or the way "Walk on the Wild Side" captures specific details of Max's Kansas City's backroom scene. Reed draws on older literary genres like the flâneur's voyeuristic slice of urban life. By contrast, Verlaine sings from within experience, narrating consciousness or confusion more than reporting specific details of what he sees. Each song, he's said, "is like a little moment of discovery or releasing something or being in a certain time or place and having a certain understanding of something."[2] Or, as Peter Laughner of the Cleveland bands Rocket from the Tombs and Pere Ubu put it, Verlaine "takes experience and abstracts it, not to the point of obscurity, but to the point of suggestion," so it's not restricted to "Verlaine's

---

2 Licht (2003).

experience per se."[3] Identifiable landmarks are few in Television songs, as are references to specific people, though the album hints at both. In this way, Verlaine's writing differs from the dominant strains of New York's poetry scene — Beats and New York School, followers of Ginsberg and O'Hara, respectively — when he and Richard Hell and Patti Smith all arrived in the late '60s, ready to write. But like the downtown scene's conceptual artists and poets, Television aimed to bring their audience along for the ride, allowing them vicariously to witness the process of a song's unfolding, to fill in spaces or gaps with their own perceptions, to contribute to the meaning being made in acts of imaginary circumambulation of a dreamy urban night.

The specifics of New York's Lower East Side poetry scene were probably not known to two kids named Richard Meyers and Tom Miller, runaways in 1966 from the Sanford School, a private prep nestled outside Wilmington, Delaware. But they knew that poets gathered in New York: Ginsberg, O'Hara, Dylan, LeRoi Jones, and others they probably hadn't even heard of. So when they showed up in New York eighteen months apart, in 1966 and 1968, they told a story about themselves that they'd run away from reform school, bound to write. Sanford had more comforts than the fugitives let on, but their parents *had* sent them there to keep them out of trouble. Both were obviously bright but not quite cut for traditional schooling, and Sanford wouldn't work out for either. Meyers had already been

---

3 Laughner (1977).

suspended once, for getting high on morning glory seeds, and the story they told of their escape from school had a distinct Beat ring to it: They stole some money from Miller's parents and headed west, first for Washington, DC, and then for Lexington, Kentucky, where Meyers had grown up and still had friends. From there: south, Florida-bound. Somewhere in Alabama they were arrested for setting fire to the field they were camping in, possibly in retribution for being harassed by rednecks. Busted, Meyers returned to his mother in Virginia but left for New York as soon as he had the cash. Miller finished high school, then flirted with college in South Carolina and Pennsylvania before dropping out and heading to find Meyers.[4] He would later say that he'd faked a suicide attempt to avoid Vietnam.[5] Meyers also convinced a military shrink that it would be in the army's interest not to draft him.[6] In New York, they worked bookstore jobs and sought out the writers and musicians they admired.

These biographical details emerge from press releases and press accounts dating from 1974–1977, stories bound up with the birth of Television, the band Meyers and Miller eventually founded together. By then, of course, they had changed their names to Hell and Verlaine. And if they colored things a little, who could blame them? The possibility for self-invention

---

4 McNeil and McCain (1996: pp. 167–8); Heylin (1993: pp. 93–4); Bell (1984).

5 Young (1977).

6 Hell (2007).

was half of New York's appeal. The Lower East Side, for young bohemians, was like a stage. Poets dressed like cowboys, strutting the streets of this urban frontier.[7] Meanwhile, the descendents of immigrant Italians, Jews, Slavs, and Puerto Ricans sheltered their children from speed freaks and a few stray hippies invading their tenements.[8] To the south and west, artists had begun to inhabit the near-abandoned Cast-iron District, a West Side neighborhood once filled with factories and warehouses, renamed SoHo in 1968.[9]

For at least a century, geographic density and low rents had made these neighborhoods conducive to artistic collaboration and cultural cross-pollination. By the time Meyers and Miller arrived, New York had witnessed several bohemian scenes in succession: As early as Herman Melville's 1852 novel *Pierre* you'll find references to "miscellaneous, bread-and-cheese adventurers, and ambiguously professional nondescripts in very genteel but shabby black." Walt Whitman was a regular at a bar called Pfaff's at Broadway and Bleecker, a meeting ground for writers, artists, and actors who published their own literary rags. An 1872 guidebook describes this neighborhood as belonging to "long-haired, queerly dressed" artists who live in attics. By 1900, provincial bohemians joined slumming Ivy Leaguers in what were still predominantly immigrant ghettos. In 1917, as the United States

---

7 Kane (2003: pp. 17–23).
8 Mele (2000: chs. 4–5).
9 Zukin (1982).

prepared to enter the Great War, the French painter Marcel Duchamp, who helped introduce New York to modern art, stood atop the Washington Square arch and declared Greenwich Village an independent republic of the mind.

That declaration renewed itself decade by decade as the neighborhood became synonymous with the idea of artistic and sexual undergrounds. By mid-century, abstract painters and New York School poets congregated at the Cedar Tavern on University Place, wresting the art world away from Paris. The rapid notoriety granted Beat poets in the late '50s led the *Village Voice*'s Norman Mailer to rhapsodize about "White Negro" hipsters. With rents rising and Italian Villagers hostile toward an influx of would-be beatniks, writers moved eastward as the '50s closed.[10] These successive scenes did not always overlap, nor did they adhere to consistent artistic or political principles, but they retained adjacent downtown neighborhoods as the site of artistic ferment.

In *Lipstick Traces*, his 1989 freewheeling "secret history" of the twentieth century, Greil Marcus unearths a punk archaeology revealing European Dadaists and mid-century Situationists as laying antiauthoritarian groundwork that would eventually crack open to reveal the Sex Pistols. Though Marcus has always shown less interest in New York's punk scene than in London's, he could have made a similar case without leaving a few square miles in downtown Manhattan. Right about the

---

10 Mele (2000: p. 142).

time Meyers and Miller were born, a handful of key artists took root downtown who, along with Ginsberg, would serve as presiding spirits over New York's underground for the next several decades. The composer John Cage moved to the Lower East Side in 1949, already having won notice for early works on prepared piano. In his courses at the New School in the late '50s and early '60s he emphasized concept as much as everyday materials in artistic production, unleashing a wave of conceptual and performance art and minimalist music, including the Fluxus movement and likeminded loft artists such as La Monte Young and Yoko Ono. From Cage and his followers, downtown musicians would inherit key artistic tenets that traced to Dada, if not to the earlier French decadents: an impulse to eliminate lines between art and life and high and low culture; a countercultural, anti-bourgeois sensibility; and a playful openness to the unknown, to chance, and to sensory derangement.[11] It's not too much of a stretch to trace lines of influence from Television back to Cage — the clear link comes through the Velvet Underground, whose members, especially John Cale, had been influenced by Cage and involved with Young's downtown minimalist movement. But it's not necessary to establish such conscious debts: as Thurston Moore of Sonic Youth, a band influenced by Television, put it: "The 'existence' of La Monte young was influential" in its own right. "I had no idea what his music sounded like until later [but] it had already changed my world

---

11 Noland (1995).

through others."[12] Even so, Verlaine had encountered Cage's influence even back in Wilmington, where as a middle schooler he had purchased, for 99 cents each, titles from *Time*'s modern music series, including work by Cage's friend Morton Feldman. He squirreled himself away in an attic room to listen, "half-asleep and half awake, . . . a totally great state of mind," he later wrote in *New York Rocker*.[13] "I played them over and over thinking, 'What's gonna happen here?' Nothing ever occurs in the usual fashion in any of these records. I can't possibly call it an influence, but it did something in terms of space, maybe."[14]

Cage's notoriety in the early '60s coincided with a revival of interest in early twentieth-century Dadaism, and especially in Marcel Duchamp. Another Duchampian, painter and Pop conceptualist Andy Warhol, also moved to Manhattan in 1949, working in commercial illustration until he established his own solo painting career in the early 1960s. Warhol's assistant, Gerard Malanga, introduced him to downtown poetry and performance circles, and though Warhol spent time on these scenes, producing cover art for small poetry journals like Ted Berrigan's *C*, he made his mark in painting and film. By 1965 he had capitalized on downtown's conceptual art gospel, making objects from ordinary life marketable in an art economy. Expanding on this concept he assumed the

---

12 Sarig (1998: p. 18).
13 Verlaine (1976).
14 Licht (2006).

role of star-maker, transforming his hangers-on into "superstars" who became famous for their proximity to him as much as for appearing in his films.

From Whitman to Warhol, the downtown avant-garde perpetuated itself through institutions like cafés, pubs, and playhouses, all friendly to conversation, performance, publication, and mind-altering substances. Beat poets preferred jazz clubs like the Five Spot on Cooper Square or coffee houses like those owned by Mickey Ruskin: the Tenth Street Coffee House (1960) and Café Les Deux Mégots, (1962). These gave way, for poets at least, to the Poetry Project at St. Mark's Church in the late '60s. Ruskin also owned a post-Cedar Tavern artists' bar, The Ninth Circle (1962). From '65 forward, another Ruskin establishment, Max's Kansas City, off Union Square, attracted a painter crowd. In 1968, when Warhol moved his studio, the Factory, from midtown to Union Square, he made the back room of Max's Kansas City *the* social destination for celebrities of all stripes.[15]

Max's Kansas City and the Poetry Project provided crucial coordinates for Meyers, Miller, and other new arrivals in the late '60s, including another aspiring poet, Patti Smith, and her sometime lover, a young photographer named Robert Mapplethorpe. The mere existence of a scene for poetry was a revelation: "[I]n Delaware, there was no 'cultural life,'" Verlaine would later say. "You might meet some guy who's four years older than you because it's your girlfriend's college

---

15 Fields (1973).

brother who might have a copy of Allen Ginsberg or something."[16] In New York, poetry readings abounded and the poetry scene provided a model of community and DIY publishing that musicians would later mimic. Meyers developed a "big crush" on local poet Bernadette Mayer, a recent New School graduate who co-edited a self-published poetry journal called *O To 9*. Meyers also idolized second-generation New York School poets such as Ted Berrigan, Anne Waldman, and Ron Padgett. Still "too shy to introduce myself to anyone," he began to model his career after these self-styled outlaws and pioneers, including Ed Sanders, a singer for the proto-punk anti-folk band the Fugs, who published his journal *Fuck You / a Magazine of the Arts* from "a secret location in the Lower East Side."[17] These poets had a profound impact on the emergence of the downtown music scene, not just in terms of style or substance, but of production mode and cultural politics: "In a way, those guys had a big influence on me in music in the sense of their attitudes towards themselves and their relationship to the existing world," Hell would recall in the mid-'90s:

> The only poets who got any attention or respect from the mainstream world were really conservative and lived their lives in universities. Rather than be frustrated and beat their heads against the wall and work their way up that system, the St. Mark's poets just stayed in the streets

---

16 Mengaziol (1981).
17 Kane (2010: p. 198).

and did it themselves on mimeo machines and created an alternative. It's just like we ended up doing in music. We made the record companies come to us by making noise for the kids directly rather than trying to impress the record companies to make deals. We brought out records on small labels and started fanzines. We created our own culture until they were forced to acknowledge it and give our records some distribution.[18]

Meyers purchased a used table-top offset printing press and launched his own journal, *Genesis : Grasp*, from an apartment on Elizabeth Street in northern Little Italy, a block off the Bowery. "Of course there is no art, only life," he announced in the manifesto that headed the first issue. The second issue was dedicated to Thomas Merton and Marcel Duchamp. The third included a Dadaist satire on philosophical criticism by Miller and Meyers on "Antilove and the Supraconscious." ("Happy trails till the next sentence!" they offer at one point. "And here I am with a personal letter for each of you. The letter U — now this is personal.") Having fallen in love with little poetry journals while working at Gotham Book Mart, Meyers sought to insert himself into this tradition.[19] A handful of Miller's poems appear in the final issue — a mixture of psychedelic imagery, violence, transcendentalism, and humor. ("all the air everywhere today enters my noses taking my breath away / I figger it's parta being a cowboy," runs one poem in its entirety.) *Genesis : Grasp* published six issues

18 Gross (1997).
19 Hell (2007).

between 1968 and 1971, and although it included poems, fiction, and photography by some recognized figures, Meyers and Miller remained marginal to the dominant scenes, something Miller seemed to resent long after he'd changed his name to Verlaine: "[P]oets would get together in various groups," he recalled, "and develop similar styles and share the same ideas and the same girlfriends. I don't know if incest is the right word, but it got to the point where everyone was just patting each other on the back and congratulating each other all the time."[20]

In addition to writing poetry — sometimes collaborating on a shared typewriter — Meyers and Miller spent their first few years in the city taking psyche-delics, "Just out of interest. To see what scrambling your senses could do to you."[21] Their bookstore jobs provided plenty of time for finding new poets and just enough money to make rent and score drugs. Occasionally they hit an artsy hotspot like Max's or the St. Adrian's, an art-ist's bar built into the same old hotel on Broadway that would house the Mercer Arts Center a few years later. On one such outing in 1969 or 1970, Meyers met Patty Oldenburg, recently separated from her husband, the Pop sculptor Claes Oldenburg. They kicked off a rela-tionship that would last close to two years. Oldenburg's husband was Meyers's senior by twenty years; Patty herself was nearly 15 years older than Meyers. The affair granted him access to downtown's elite art circles.

---

20 Heylin (1993: p. 98).
21 Verlaine, in Heylin (1993: p. 96); see also Robinson (1977).

Meyers, in turn, published her poems in *Genesis : Grasp* under the pseudonym Patty Machine, along with such noted poets as Clark Coolidge and Bruce Andrews. The magazine was Meyers's attempt to "fashion a community of writers into which I fit," he later said.[22] His own poems sometimes appeared under the name Ernie Stomach. He and Miller collaborated under the pseudonym Theresa Stern, whose "photo" — a composite of their faces, crowned with a dark wig — graced the cover of *Genesis : Grasp*'s final issue, along with portraits of Rimbaud and Artaud. Two years later, when Hell issued a volume of Theresa Stern's poetry entitled *Wanna Go Out?*, a biographical statement described her as a half-German, half-Puerto Rican Hoboken hooker whose date of birth fell in the few weeks that separated Hell's from Verlaine's at the end of 1949. That collaboration would be their last strictly poetic effort together; by the time *Wanna Go Out?* appeared, Meyers and Miller had shifted their sights to rock 'n' roll.

Downtown's music scene, on Meyers and Miller's arrival, divided into leftover folk utopians and an experimental underground scene influenced by Cage and his followers. The former, in spite of their countercultural politics, had spawned enormous commercial successes such as Baez and Dylan, and by mid-decade had seen Dylan defect to rock 'n' roll. Dylan epitomized the transforming power of image as he cultivated his own mystique, first as folk troubadour, then as rock's

---

22 Melillo (2009: p. 65).

coolest cat. Touted outside the academy as a poet, he sought out ties to Beat heroes, which they reciprocated. The back cover to *Bringing It All Back Home* (1965) uses photos of Ginsberg to establish Dylan's poetic credentials, and in D. A. Pennebaker's film *Don't Look Back*, which follows Dylan through a 1965 tour of England, Ginsberg hovers over the setpiece for "Subterranean Homesick Blues," an authorizing force. Dylan's break from the Village folk scene — "fat people," he famously dismissed them — was a turn toward hipster cool, influencing not only the Velvets' post-Beat image but later musicians as well. When Dylan performed "Like A Rolling Stone" and other electric songs in Manchester, England, in 1966, and an audience member called him out as a "Judas" to the folk movement, Dylan responded by telling his band to play the song "fucking loud." In that performance we hear one origin point of a disposition that would later be recognized as punk. Richard Hell took this version of Dylan as an inspiration: "I knew him for the first electric records he made and I was so full of aggression myself when I first started playing music that I really didn't understand anything else. I wanted music that just RIPPED through you."[23]

While Dylan forced the folk scene's identity crisis, other musicians pioneered forms that would later prove significant to Television's development. Inspired by Cage, younger underground artists, beginning in 1959, staged downtown events known as Happenings, which

---

23 Hell (1997).

combined art forms — dance, theater, film, poetry, music, sculpture — in multimedia events that smudged lines between artists and audiences.[24] On one hand, Happenings pointed to the theatricality of everyday life; on the other, they made art more democratic. Some of the work that emerged from these contexts — especially Pop art — came to be commercially viable, though much of it willfully resisted commodification.

Warhol, who never pretended his work existed outside a commercial realm, oversaw the combination of rock 'n' roll and Happenings when he incorporated the largely unknown Velvet Underground into multimedia, amphetamine-fueled spectacles he dubbed Andy Warhol's Exploding Plastic Inevitable.[25] But even earlier, he and other artists attempted to incorporate popular music into Pop. In 1963 the Oldenburgs unsuccessfully tried to form a band, with Patty as lead singer. Andy Warhol and artist Lucas Samaras would sing backup, with painter Larry Poons on guitar, sculptor Walter de Maria on drums, and composer La Monte Young on saxophone. The painter Jasper Johns would contribute lyrics.[26] The group folded because Young had no interest in entertainment or commercial culture, but De Maria would later play in a short-lived rock band, the Primitives, with filmmaker and composer Tony Conrad and violist John Cale, both of whom also worked with Young. The Primitives

---

24 Banes (1993: p. 55–8); Kaprow (1961).
25 DeRogatis (2009: pp. 62–72).
26 Grunenberg and Harris (2005: p. 242).

formed to promote a novelty dance single written by 22-year-old Lou Reed, with whom Cale would go on to form the Velvet Underground, whose rock 'n' roll referenced downtown avant-garde predecessors.[27] Unlike Young, these artists felt that pop music — like other forms of culture appropriated, satirized, and celebrated by Pop Art — was a field rife with artistic opportunities.

For years after their breakup, the Velvets served as the benchmark of New York's rock underground, in spite of the fact that they never reached mainstream audiences. Local radio offered no support. Once Warhol's media experiments had expired, the band looked elsewhere for an audience, spending the end of the '60s on the road. Many listeners, even sympathetic ones like Richard Williams of the British music paper *Melody Maker*, found their music "hard, ugly, and based on a kind of sadomasochistic world which few dared enter," though Williams, for one, heralded their music as superior to *Sgt. Pepper*.[28] The Velvets' commercial failure would be attributed to their artistic integrity, since they rejected commercial radio format for representational practices — and subject matter — required by narrative and artistic agendas they set for themselves. The Velvets' ill-fated career arc set a template for Television's, as would the influence they eventually exerted on subsequent generations of musicians.

27 Joseph (2002); Bockris and Malanga (1983: p. 13).
28 Williams (2005: pp. 119, 121).

When Lou Reed played his final shows with the Velvet Underground at Max's in the summer of 1970, a vacuum opened downtown. Warhol himself had been scarce since an attempted assassination in '68. His party crowd still hung out. But what would it take as an organizing principle? The answer would come soon enough, flamboyant and covered in glitter, and the UK's music and culture tabloids, addicted to Dylan and fearing they had come too late to the Velvets, would be in the right place to welcome it with arms open. Verlaine would later claim that CBGB's bands "shared a dislike for '70s bands, which may have included — besides bands like the Eagles and the Bee Gees — even the New York Dolls and that glamour rock crap."[29] But a closer look at the downtown scene throughout CBGB's early years suggests plentiful continuities between New York's glitter and nascent punk scenes. Television owed a greater debt to these camp nostalgists than is often assumed.

---

29 Verlaine (1976).

2
Downtown Satyricon

The back room at Max's is a dimly lit, red-table-clothed, 20 by 20 foot den of iniquity. The food's not much, and the drinks aren't cheap, but no one really goes there to drink or eat; they go to see and be seen.
— *Dave Marsh*, Melody Maker, *6 October 1973*

Marquee Moon bears faint traces of what the cultural historian Andreas Killen calls "Warholism": the replacement of pre-'60s certainties about American life with "nostalgia, camp, and irony, the claustrophobic minutae of life inside the media echo chamber."[1] Television itself, however, was born directly under a Warholian sign, as was much of the music in the '70s downtown scene. Warhol broke down barriers between high and low culture, injected the underground into the mainstream, made life into performance art. Rock 'n' roll seemed a logical medium for this project, but Warholism extended far

---

1 Killen (2006: p. 138).

beyond the limited reach of the underground, Velvet or otherwise. Dylan's career offers an even more visible example of celebrity's transformative force. If he was the patron saint of celebrity cool, Warhol was its theologian, and the Factory and Max's Kansas City were its sacred spaces. There, identity transformations like those Dylan had repeatedly undergone took even more extreme forms, as Warhol surrounded himself with drag queens who laid bare the degree to which all identity, including gender, was performed. As Mary Harron wrote in 1980, looking back over an explosive two decades, Warhol had helped to create "an attitude" in New York, "tough, funny, sharp-witted — sustained by many of [his] superstars even when they were showing their scars. It was the attitude of people who had been through the mill and come out flaunting. Their detachment, the way they parodied themselves, was a form of courage — and if you were a drag queen in 1966, you needed all the courage you could get." When Richard Hell, writing in CBGB's early days, declared that "celebrity-hood" would be "the art form of the future," he had similar principles in mind.[2]

The mass media fusion of life and celebrity characterized the downtown scene in the early '70s, as did a parodic impulse that sealed off the scene from aggressive politicking like John Lennon's. Following Warhol's example of "*consciously* developing an image," a pattern Bowie followed spectacularly as Ziggy Stardust, savvy

2 Heylin (1993: p. 240).

downtown artists sought to use the media before they were used by them.[3] Hell would follow this blueprint in Television's founding, benefitting from local and international media interest in New York's art and music undergrounds. Max's back room was filled not only with artists and musicians, but also with critics and producers, a network of individuals with transatlantic influence who would cultivate a series of underground scenes leading up to the advent of Television and CBGB's heyday. In the words of Danny Goldberg, journalist and later a record exec, this clique sought to function as a "collective conscience" that would "maintain the integrity of the rock culture" by promoting artists they believed had "authentic talent and energy."[4]

Chief among this clique were Lisa and Richard Robinson, a journalist and an A&R man, and Danny Fields, an A&R man-turned-editor at *16* magazine. The three of them had introduced Bowie to Iggy Pop, Lou Reed, and the Warhol crowd in the fall of 1971. Fields had signed the MC5 and the Stooges to Elektra in the late '60s and had then managed the latter. Richard Robinson had engineered Lou Reed's solo debut. A transatlantic columnist for *NME*, Lisa Robinson also edited *Hit Parader* magazine (a mainstream music monthly), wrote a cheeky rock fashion column for the Detroit-based *Creem*, and in 1973 founded *Rock Scene* magazine — which featured "a very camp sensibility but also a very New York sensibility" — with

---

3 Harron (1980).
4 Goldberg (2008: pp. 30, 29).

her husband and guitarist Lenny Kaye, specifically to promote unsigned New York bands.[5]

Like Tom Miller, Richard Meyers, and many other downtowners, from 1972 to 1975 these scenemakers were fans and ready advocates of a new band, the New York Dolls. Street smart, christened in Max's back room, they combined the raw sound of early Who with Mick Jagger's cocky swagger, all in a New York accent and injected with the campy glamour of Warhol's drag stars. Though they were more or less straight, the Dolls played great stage queens, taking underground drag antics on stage, on vinyl, and eventually on the road. David Johansen and Johnny Thunders sometimes looked like they were about to make out while sharing a mic, and Johansen regularly waxed sibilant and flung a limp wrist for effect. On occasion — for interviews, photo shoots, their album cover, and some live shows — they dressed in drag. They also rocked like a Long Island rec room circa '66, and on that score, they pushed glam's fascination with '30s glamour — a campy return to the world of cabaret — firmly into rock 'n' roll territory. Beginning in June '72, they played a 17-week residency at the Mercer, whose more high-minded avant-garde owners hoped the Dolls' trashy but growing following would help them make rent. Though Television would present itself two years later as an overt rejection of glitter, Hell and Verlaine initially took the Dolls as inspiration, and *Marquee Moon* itself bears discernable traces of Warhol's and the Dolls' downtown reigns.

---

5 Lisa Robinson, in Gorman (2001: p. 146).

As Max's and Mercer's regulars, the Robinsons and Fields knew Patti Smith, who would become another force central to Television's development. A relentless scene-crosser a few years older than Meyers and Miller, Smith had come to New York just after Meyers, in 1967, also aiming to be a poet. Breaking into underground theater first, she appeared in the gender-bending burlesque *Femme Fatale* (1969), written by Jackie Curtis and featuring a Warholian menagerie: Wayne County, Penny Arcade, and Mary Woronov. Staged at the East Village experimental theater La MaMa, Curtis's play was produced under the aegis of the Theater of the Ridiculous, a company whose works centered on gender and sexuality and routinely featured Warhol types. Smith would perform in other plays, including *Cowboy Mouth*, which she co-wrote with Obie-winner Sam Shepard, with whom she was having an affair.

A few months prior to her performance with Shepard, in February 1971 Smith gave a reading at the Poetry Project while Lenny Kaye improvised on electric guitar behind her. She was opening for the poet Gerard Malanga, Warhol's downtown guide in the early '60s and whip-dancer in the Exploding Plastic Inevitable. Smith and Malanga pulled together several disparate threads of the downtown performing arts scene to create a who's-who audience: poets (including Ginsberg) and musicians (Dylan's friend Bobby Neuwirth), fashion models, rock journalists and industry types (including the Robinsons and Fields), other Max's regulars (including Warhol assistant Terry Ork), along with Theater of the Ridiculous personnel.[6] Kaye had his own connections: he was the music editor for the men's magazine *Cavalier*, a regular contributor to *Rolling Stone*, and occasionally, like Patti, to *Creem*.

Smith deftly bridged the gap between downtown poetry and cabaret. She kicked off her reading with a performance of "Mack the Knife" in honor of Bertholt Brecht, then dedicated the rest of the evening to "all that is criminal, the great pit of Babel," to Hell itself. Though she left the camp at the door — no one is more serious about Brecht and Weill than Patti Smith — she shared Theater of the Ridiculous obsessions with gender and religion. Her own tagphrase before long would be "beyond gender," anticipating one of the keynotes of the post-Stonewall downtown scene.

Smith wouldn't perform again with Kaye for another two years. In the meantime she appeared in a Saks fashion show wearing a ratty T-shirt (later cited as an inspiration by Richard Hell), was featured in *Andy Warhol's Interview*, published four poetry chapbooks, opened regularly for glitter bands at the Mercer, and held two more solo readings at the Poetry Project. She published rock criticism and traveled to London with Malanga for a reading that received attention for Malanga's connection with the Velvets. Smith's poetry revealed her obsessions with rock stars; her criticism, like that of *Creem*'s Lester Bangs, was unabashedly autobiographical, reveling in her admiration for the Stones, Hendrix, Dylan. In late '73 she and

---

6 Bockris and Bayley (1999: pp. 13–18).

Kaye reunited for a "Rock n Rimbaud" extravaganza, celebrating the life and death of the French poet in a show at Les Jardins, a new gay discotheque on the rooftop of the Hotel Diplomat on W. 43rd St. For an audience full of Warhol's inner circle, she and Kaye laid down a combination of French decadent poetry and rock 'n' roll that was already, unknown to her, percolating through Television's earliest songs in their Chinatown rehearsal space.

Smith's relationship with Kaye had been spurred by a piece he'd written on Philly and South Jersey doo-wop. She contacted him through the Robinsons and the two made fast friends, spinning old 45s and dancing through the aisles of Village Oldies records, where Kaye worked.[7] Kaye's music interests were broad and deep, philosophical and historical. In 1972, he convinced Elektra to issue *Nuggets*, a double LP of hard-to-find '60s garage singles. The compilation of songs Kaye described as "punk rock" has been credited with fueling the revival of interest in garage-psych sounds such as the 13th Floor Elevators' "You're Gonna Miss Me" and the Count Five's "Psychotic Reaction," which resonated with the New York Dolls' energy and would also influence early Television.

It didn't take long for the Dolls to register with the same London press that obsessed over Iggy, Bowie, Reed, and, before them, Dylan. Their first UK tour ended disastrously that November when their drummer overdosed in a fan's bathtub, piping-hot coffee

---

7 Fletcher (2009: pp. 301–2).

poured down his gullet while he was out. When they'd recouped and hit the road again, the Dolls perplexed American audiences outside urban areas. *Creem* sent Lisa Robinson to cover the tour, where she witnessed enthusiastic, lipschticked fans in LA but apprehension at most stops between coasts. Fields, also along for the ride, saw the Dolls as theater more than an actual band: "Anyone connected with this industry who talks about music, well that's just astonishing," he told Robinson for her *Creem* piece. "Play music indeed — thank God they don't have to."[8]

Talent or no, the Dolls inspired Meyers and Miller to form their own band, the Neon Boys, with Tom's old Delaware bandmate, Billy Ficca, on drums. Ficca also shared Miller's penchant for free jazz, especially for Tony Williams, who had drummed with the Miles Davis Quintet and would pioneer jazz-rock fusion. (Davis called him "one of the baddest motherfuckers who had ever played a set of drums.") Though they never performed, the Neon Boys demoed a handful of tracks in early '73. Meyers's songs — "Love Comes In Spurts," "That's All I Know (Right Now)," and "High Heeled Wheels" — featured slightly sneering vocals, Dylan crossed with David Johansen, delivered over jangly guitar lines, like Lou Reed playing early Who. Like Miller's songs ("Tramp," "Hot Dog," and "Poor Circulation"), the demos of which remain unreleased, most of Meyers's compositions would make it onto early Television setlists. Unsatisfied with their

---

8 Cagle (1995: p. 189).

sound, however, the band sat on the recordings and advertised for a second guitarist in the *Voice* and *Creem*: "Narcissistic rhythm guitarist wanted — minimal talent okay." Respondents included Chris Stein, who would later play for the Stillettoes and Blondie, and Doug Colvin, later Dee Dee Ramone, but the band couldn't settle on someone they liked and soon dissolved. Ficca moved to Boston. Verlaine would later say that he and Hell had already experienced creative differences over his distaste for Hell's vocals.[9]

To understand the world the Neon Boys hoped to enter, consider a scene piece written by the 22-year-old journalist Nick Kent, who'd been sent by *NME* that spring to report on the post-Velvets underground that had spawned the Dolls. Kent was perfect for the job. He holed up at the infamous Chelsea Hotel and made the rounds of downtown hotspots. The article he eventually published, though, brims with disappointment. Max's wasn't nearly as seedy as legend had it. (Even the bathroom graffiti is boring, he complains.) The crowd consisted of "city boys in denims . . . toting their Jack Kerouac post-beatnik complexes." Kent homes in on Eric Emerson, a pony-tailed "ex-Warhol extra" who looks "like a reject from Paul Revere and the Raiders." Emerson and the Magic Tramps epitomize what Kent calls "the new-wave New York bizarro-bands that sprout from the more bohemian areas of the Big Apple," a cluster of bands whose sound Kent traces to the mid-'60s Long Island white-boy R&B bands such as the Young Rascals,

9 Verlaine (1976).

the Vagrants, and the "punk-mysterioso" Vanilla Fudge. This garage band tradition, Kent explains, opened the door to the Velvet Underground.[10]

In establishing these lines of influence, Kent's piece lays important groundwork for Television's entrance on the downtown scene. By 1973 the Velvets had come and gone, but Reed still served as a dysfunctional god-father to a nascent glitter scene, "smiling benignly if a little hazily down on the latest developments of the downtown Satyricon."[11] Kent, like Lester Bangs, was as put off by Reed's new incarnation as he'd been drawn to the Velvets' mystique. Reed had been a dirtier, under-ground version of the snarling proto-punk Dylan but now was a shallow parody of himself: stoned, bloated, easily bowled over by Bowie.[12]

Reed's *Transformer*-era transformation made sense given the modulations the downtown scene itself had undergone: his celebration of Warhol's drag superstars in "Walk on the Wild Side" was essentially a New York School poem, cliquishly self-referential to the initiated, set to a radio-friendly pop pastiche. Kent thought the Dolls-centered downtown scene couldn't decide whether to revive '60s rock or parody it in a drag revue. Reed's hit song expressed this ambivalence: it was the "very own anthem" of the Max's scene, a product of the '60s underground that still, somehow, would be fit for cabaret divas like Streisand or Midler

10 Kent (1973b).
11 Kent (1973b).
12 Cf. Bangs (1973).

to cover: "I think Bette Midler could absolutely tear it up," Kent wrote.[13]

The idea of Midler covering Reed isn't as far-fetched as it might seem today. The "Divine Miss M" had cut her chops at Hilly Kristal's pre-CBGB clubs and at gay bath houses on the Upper West Side, where the Dolls also played in the summer of '72. Invoking her in relation to Reed was a nod to Reed's sexual ambiguity in the early '70s. But Kent's comment also nodded to downtown's cabaret revival, combining '60s nightclub settings (previously dominated by folk and jazz) with influences from Happenings, the Theater of the Ridiculous, and a longer underground drag tradition to establish a decadent Weimar aesthetic as the city and nation seemed poised to crumble amidst financial crisis and political corruption.

Like the Dolls, Patti Smith was a natural fit for this cabaret scene. Following several solo readings opening for bands the Mercer in '72, she and Lenny Kaye followed their "Rock n Rimbaud" event with a string of dates opening for folk veteran Phil Ochs at Max's and another run in April '74 supporting the Warhol drag star Holly Woodlawn at the Village supper club Reno Sweeney. This nostalgic cabaret club, founded in 1973, catered to what the *Times* called "the traditional supper-club mix of porky businessmen and garment-center models, show-business fringe characters, willowy men and short-haired women."[14] Its Paradise Room was, like Max's and like the Mercer, a place to be seen,

---

13 Kent (1973c).
14 Buckley (1973).

though an upscale version that tended toward more straightforward show tunes for a mixed gay/straight, uptown/downtown audience. Its owners had hoped Midler would headline their opening, though she already beyond their reach.[15] Smith's interests ran to cabaret's darker side — Weill and Lenya — celebrations of subterranean decadence. She brought to Reno Sweeney a proto-punk edge that didn't undermine her sincere appreciation of the cabaret genre.

The confluence of downtown scenes Kent witnessed in '73 — cabaret, glitter, and garage revival — had the unlikely effect of spawning punk rock. Meyers and Miller had been particularly energized by the Mercer's '73 New Year's celebration, featuring Suicide, the Modern Lovers, Wayne County, and the Dolls. Hell recalled a "hysterical" audience, "very campy, lots of gorgeous young girls, too, all in mini-skirts and platforms and feather boas, heavy make-up."[16] It occurred to him that "there was so much more excitement in rock & roll [than] sitting home writing poetry . . . I mean I could deal with the same matters that I'd be sweating over alone in my room, to put out little mimeograph magazines that five people would ever see. And we definitely thought we were as cool as the next people, so why not get out there and sell it?"[17] What he saw at the Mercer directly contrasted corporate rock: "Music had just become so bloated,"

15 Gavin (2006: chs. 9–10).
16 Mitchell (2006: p. 29).
17 McNeil and McCain (1996: p. 163).

he'd recall. "With the Dolls, it was just like the street put onstage, you know?"[18] Being on stage, he implies, didn't have to be artificial. He'd make a paradoxical stage presence by performing authenticity.

The friends' second attempt to break into the scene came when Miller, with Meyers as manager, auditioned at Reno Sweeney in October 1973. Miller and Meyers seemed an unlikely match for the supper club, though perhaps Meyers hoped to pass off Miller, like Patti Smith, as a streetwise version of glossier cabaret acts. Lloyd would later claim that Meyers ripped Miller's shirt on his way in, hoping to make him look "ragged." When Miller plugged in his guitar on stage, the volume was up so loud that the amplifier popped, sending the manager scurrying over in a panic.[19]

Miller's 15-minute audition at Reno Sweeney consisted of three songs, one of which, "Venus de Milo," would later appear on *Marquee Moon*. The owners hated him, but the audience that night included two people who would help bring Television into existence. Terry Ork, a Warhol assistant and Max's regular, was a friend of Smith and Mapplethorpe's and was Meyers and Miller's boss at Cinemabilia, a 12th Street bookstore devoted to film titles. He'd brought along Richard Lloyd, a young guitarist with bottle-blond Iggy Poppet bowl cut and, on occasion, pink lipstick, who'd been splitting time between Ork's loft and Danny Fields's, having just arrived from LA.

---

18 McNeil and McCain (1996: p. 119).
19 Mitchell (2006: p. 34).

Lloyd had met Ork at Max's, where he'd headed to sniff out scenesters he'd met out West, including the photographer Leee Black Childers. Childers had singled out Lloyd in an LA audience for British glam rockers Mott the Hoople and invited him, based on looks, to a backstage party. Lloyd parlayed the connection into a stint sleeping at Fields's when he arrived back in New York. At some point he started crashing at Ork's Chinatown loft. Years later he'd refer to Ork as having been his "lover," then quickly qualify: "Oh, he wasn't, he just chased me around."[20] Hilly Kristal recalled Ork as a "pudgy little dynamo with a penchant for non-stop talking."[21] Ork aspired to be like the Robinsons and Fields, like Warhol, even. A behind-the-scenes conduit, he enjoyed making connections. Earlier he'd introduced Patti Smith to Malanga.[22] Now he suggested that Miller and Lloyd form a band. He'd buy equipment and offer his space for rehearsals. Miller and Meyers phoned up Ficca in Boston and asked him to come back. After flirting with various names (including the Libertines and Goo Goo) they settled on Television, a name Meyers suggested. "It's so obtrusive, it's unobtrusive," Lloyd would later say.[23] What better symbol of an era than the medium that threatened to absorb all others?

---

20 "Richard Lloyd, Man on the Marquee Moon" (2009).
21 Kristal, "The History of CBGB & OMFUG."
22 McNeil and McCain (1996: p. 106).
23 Gholson (1976).

3
Stunned into an Electric Metaphor

Rock music, which came of age with television, is totally obsessed by personality.
— *Mary Harron*, Melody Maker, *February 1980*

What came first and foremost to Television was mystique.
— *Craig Gholson*, New York Rocker, *March 1977*

Certain New York scene residents recall being placed under the distinct impression that Hell was of some dark German ancestry (as opposed to the tame reality of a Kentucky upbringing) and that Verlaine was possibly a product of some obscure Gallic nobility, though it remains to be seen whether this was just wishful thinking on the part of spectators instead of a knowing ploy conducted by the two young artists.
— *Nick Kent*, NME, *March 1977*

In August 1973, two months before Miller and Meyers met Lloyd at Reno Sweeney, the old Broadway Central

Hotel, which housed the Mercer Arts Center, collapsed. Eric Emerson and the Magic Tramps were rehearsing inside and escaped unharmed; the Dolls were up at Madison Square Garden, preparing to open that night for Mott the Hoople. The Broadway side of old hotel simply sagged and fell, spilling tons of debris into the street and burying four welfare tenants in the rubble.[1] It's hard not to view the event, in retrospect, as a handy organizational device, a dividing line between glitter and punk, though that line is not so neat, and by the time *Marquee Moon* was recorded three years later the new mythology surrounding Television's discovery of CBGB's served also to divide an early CB's scene from a late one. Either you were at CB's from the beginning or you'd arrived a little too late. And nobody was there as early as Television, or so the story would go.

In retrospect, things would seem to fall into place almost effortlessly. Meyers and Miller changed their names to Hell and Verlaine; they played a debut show in a small theater near Times Square; and then one or more of the band members chanced upon a crummy little club on the Bowery. The rest, as a *Boston Phoenix* writer put it in 1977, was already "punk rock history":

> The first press notice [for Television] — a rave by Patti Smith in the *Soho Weekly News*; the Tom and Patti liaison that followed; the dispute with Richard Hell and his replacement by Fred Smith, the bassist from Blondie;

---

1 Fletcher (2009: p. 322).

the Patti Smith/Television double bill in the spring of 1975 that established CBGB's as the avant-garde rock hangout *sans pareil*; and the rapid development of a complete CBGB's scene, with CBGB's bands, a CBGB's fan mag and, of course, a CBGB's record.[2]

But at the start of 1974, all this was prospect, and though the venues were shifting (literally, in the case of the Mercer), what started at CBGB's was less a new scene than what one friend of Debbie Harry's band, the Stillettoes, later described as "the heavy tail end of glitter."[3] It was still the Age of Warhol, and that meant presenting a carefully choreographed image, one that would lend itself to legend.

With some rehearsal down, the band began to cultivate its identity, sonically and conceptually. They rejected glitter's nostalgia for the '30s in favor of a post-apocalyptic take on rough '50s street style. Sonically, Lloyd brought exactly what the Neon Boys had lacked. Born outside Pittsburgh, a couple years younger than his bandmates, Lloyd had grown up in Pennsylvania, New Jersey, and New York, playing drums and piano before settling on guitar. Living in Greenwich Village and attending Manhattan's Stuyvesant High School, Lloyd honed his axe skills, imitating heroes like Jeff Beck and Hendrix, the latter of whom he met once through a friend and watched once or twice in studio.[4] He also took inspiration, he would say on the eve of

---

2 Rose (1977).
3 Anya Phillips, in Bangs (1980: p. 19).
4 Dery (1988); Gerstenzang (2009); Wildsmith (2009).

Marquee Moon's release, from the "primitive electric blues" of Buddy Guy, Magic Sam, and Elmore James. Before he'd made much of his talent, though, a bad drug trip in Times Square landed him in a psychiatric hospital — "tied down for two weeks once and I thought flying saucers were landing"[5] — a stint he followed up by skipping town and traveling to Boston and LA, where he hung around local music scenes.

Lloyd churned out rough rhythm guitar and bluesy riffs; when he soloed he tended, like Beck, toward volatility, pushing from untamed noodling into new, ethereal spheres. Verlaine, by contrast, provided governing shapes and structure, sounding out foundational patterns that would play off one another, balance, unbalance, repeat. His solos shredded single-string tremolos and scrambled-up scales, improvisations testing the terrain one dissonant step at a time. From the start he showed a preference for old-school Fenders (Verlaine helped launch a Jazzmaster revival), creating clean sounds, thick but precise. On occasion he would lose control in a free jazz barrage, evidence of his early admiration for Albert Ayler, Tony Williams, the New York Art Quartet, and especially the guitarist John McLaughlin, who like Verlaine soaked free-range solos in chilly harmonics.[6]

Most early Television numbers were firmly in the *Nuggets* vein: 4/4 signatures (though never four-to-the-floor boogies), thumping bass from Hell, trebly

---

5 Gholson (1976).
6 Kugel (1977).

guitar lines and urgent ascensions. Verlaine's vocals were adenoidal and anguished. Kristal's memories of Television's first shows as terrible may have been accurate, judging from footage of loft rehearsals taken sometime in '74. The band's energy discernibly derives from the Velvets' "Sister Ray" or the Elevators' more frenetic side. If they retained psychedelic traces, as critics would frequently suggest, they mixed San Francisco sounds with Music Machine's testosterone-fuelled, bass-heavy "Talk Talk" or the Count Five's "Psychotic Reaction," the latter of which they covered in early sets. Several songs filmed in Ork's loft disintegrate into noise, and one, "Eat the Light," includes a miserable attempt at group harmony, but true gems stand out, including a rough version of a rather sweet song called "What I Heard" with vocals by Lloyd. (Its tune and arrangement would reappear years later as Verlaine's "Postcard from Waterloo.")

The rehearsal tapes reveal Television's continuities with the Mercers scene. The Dolls' "Personality Crisis" blares in the background at one point, presumably as inspiration. Hell and Lloyd reveled in rock theatricality from the start, swiveling hips, taking Townshend leaps, Lloyd kicking back platformed heels on the offbeat. Verlaine's unique vocals have glam antecedents: they shared ground with Dylan and Neil Young, sure, but tonally relied more on Reed, Pop, and Johansen, often with the same drag queen attitude that Reed pulled on the Warhol-inspired "Vicious," or Iggy had unleashed even earlier on "Loose." That campy sneer, like Wayne County's and David Johansen's the offspring of Mick Jagger, suggests Television's commonalities with glitter's sound if not style: well into 1975, Verlaine would preface early versions of "Foxhole" with a suggestive "*Hey*, soldier boy . . ." The song "Eat the Light," with its harmonies that never cohered, has the girl-group call-and-response structure that would resurface in "See No Evil" and "Venus." Some early tunes, though, broke the glitter-garage mold. Many clocked in at under four minutes, suggesting early punk's enshrinement of primitive rock, but a few stretch past five minutes. These early rehearsal tapes reveal songs ("Horizontal Ascension," "Change Your Channels") that already eschew radio-single formats for wandering introductions and choruses that build toward drawn-out climaxes.

In the Age of Warhol, surface was substance, and Television's visual image was initially more coherent than its music. Hell crafted Television's anti-glitter image prior to the band's debut, suggesting a clean break from the old scene, a cleaner break than the sound would suggest by itself. Hell's '50s street style set the stage for the Ramones' variation on the theme. When Lloyd re-encountered Leee Back Childers in New York and invited him to a Television rehearsal, the photographer sensed the coming revolution. He'd thought of the glitter scene, including the Dolls, as an extension of "the Theatre of the Ridiculous, it was the same people — more as an art movement" than as a music scene, he told Jon Savage in the late '80s. "Shortly thereafter, when Patti Smith started up, I still looked at it as a theatrical thing, a poetry thing."

But watching Television rehearse he sensed something else: "[I]t was very rough, very weird, but very different. That was the first time I realized the thing I was thinking of theatrically could in fact become rock 'n' roll. I loved Television from that time on."[7]

Television's image called for a set of new names. Having dabbled with pseudonyms in their poetry, Meyers and Miller didn't have to stretch for the idea of crafting rock personalities. Moreover, renaming themselves on the inauguration of a new artistic career had an obvious precedent in Robert Zimmerman's transformation into Bob Dylan. Like Dylan, Meyers and Miller would replace their given surnames with loaded literary references: if Zimmerman had aligned himself with Dylan Thomas, Meyers reached back even further for his patronym: his new name, "Hell," paid homage to Rimbaud's *Une Saison en Enfer* on the centennial of that bohemian lodestone's publication.

Rimbaud had been a key figure for Ginsberg, O'Hara, Burroughs, and Dylan (who in '75 would name-check Verlaine and Rimbaud, rhyming the latter with the title of "You're Going to Make Me Lonesome When You Go"), as he had been for Dadaists and surrealists even earlier and was for contemporaries such as Reed, Smith, Mapplethorpe, and Carroll. In the spring of '74, just as Television was gearing up to go public, Rimbaud and Verlaine were on New York's cultural radar as the subject of Christopher Hampton's play *Total Eclipse*, which held a steady run at the Brooklyn

---

7 Savage (2010: p. 85).

Academy of Music's Chelsea Theater. For all these artists, Rimbaud was a metonym for decadence, the way
Blake was a metonym for Romantic vision or Whitman
for sexual liberation. As recently as 2008, reviewing
a Rimbaud biography for the *Times*, Hell brims with
youthful enthusiasm when he describes Rimbaud's
rebellion as "a function of his peasant, punkish ultra-
confidence in the value of his pure (unegotistic) honesty,
as an adolescent seeing through the adult hypocrisy
and convention veiling the sensual, unsane world."[8]
Reading Hell writing about Rimbaud, it's hard not to
sense lingering autobiographical reverberations.

Miller renamed himself too. His comments on the
process came long after Hell left Television, and should
be so qualified: "It was this very conscious decision on
one level," he told *NME*'s Nick Kent after *Marquee
Moon*'s release.

> We just felt that we had to change our names in order to
> make a mark — though mostly it was done just for fun,
> now I recall. Richard had already chosen his name —
> Hell as much for the sound as for its implications
> (laughs). And for my name . . . I had a list of, oh, at least
> 30 names down and we were both just going through
> them when I mentioned "Verlaine." Richard thought
> it sounded fantastic — y'know, "Wow that's a fantastic
> name! Use that one," so that really clinched it. I just
> liked the sound of it. That's all.[9]

---

8 Hell (2008).
9 Kent (1977b).

The slight defensiveness suggests exasperation only a few years after taking on a new identity. He showed similar impatience when asked whether the band name was "punning on Tom's adopted initials?" "'Maybe, I dunno,' Verlaine hedges. He's clearly bored with the joke."[10] Elsewhere Verlaine waxed philosophical:

> It was just some kind of way of disassociating yourself from your own past, a way to be something that you want to be . . . You didn't have any choice in your name when you were born, so you realize that, and then figure out maybe you do have a choice.[11]

The nod to self-invention aligns Verlaine with Hell's desire to return to rock 'n' roll "the knowledge that you invent yourself."[12] In their renaming, the choice of Verlaine and Rimbaud as antecedents was hardly accidental: they were a pair, perhaps literary history's most famous gay lovers. The title of Rimbaud's *A Season in Hell* refers to their tempestuous, violent, dragging-themselves-drunk-through-the-streets relationship. At one point Verlaine had fired shots at Rimbaud, who had him arrested on attempted murder charges and examined to evaluate his sanity. This dimension of their relationship, fundamental to their legendary stature, seems to have been on Hell's radar. (His fascination with the Verlaine-Rimbaud romance would resurface in his 2005 novel *Godlike*, set in the

---

10 Strick (1976).
11 Heylin (1993: p. 117).
12 Heylin (1993: p. 118).

East Village poetry scene of the early '70s.) Though not romantic or sexual, Hell and Verlaine's relationship had an intensity that made them seem a pair. Note, for instance, that the other two band members didn't feel compelled to change their names as well.

Hell's and Verlaine's new names resonated with the atmosphere of sexual decadence that had reigned in downtown bohemian enclaves for decades but had been especially intense, and visible, on the glitter scene. For Tom's part, as Ork made plain, the post-Bowie vogue for bisexuality that ran through the downtown satyricon wasn't in the picture: "He was just so tightly wound," Ork says in *Please Kill Me*.

> He was always concerned about men coming on to him. I mean, he was pretty, but I think he didn't really know what life was about. He had just accrued experience from books — it was all read, and not lived. He was very naïve in a lot of ways. As opposed to Richard Hell, who had both feet in the ooze.[13]

(Ork, Hell, and Lloyd all developed heroin habits in the '70s; heroin, in Roberta Bayley's recollection, organized a secret society within the downtown scene.[14]) McNeil and McCain juxtapose Ork's comments on Verlaine with Ork's and Fields's effusions about Richard Lloyd, who played the role of Television's requisite male hustler: Ork said he'd been "in love" with Lloyd,

---

13 McNeil and McCain (1996: p. 167).
14 Savage (2010: p. 139).

who was "certainly even more 'lived' than Hell or Verlaine." Nick Kent, shortly after *Marquee Moon*'s release, thumb-nailed Lloyd as having a "pretty-boy pout to his features that apparently was most appealing to the gay community."[15] Fields played to the same tune: "Everybody fucked Richard Lloyd. He was another one with gorgeous skin. He was another gorgeous beauty. It was the band of beauties."[16] Though Lloyd would later complain that McNeil had reduced eight hours of interviews to their most lurid residue, he still seemed pleased at having been designated the band's bisexual darling: "The wonderful thing in *Please Kill Me*," he said years later, "is that I so come across as though everyone is all talking about 'how much they loved me.' So it's a stroke to my vanity."[17] Who needed to change names to try on a new identity?

Now for the new look: Hell cut his hair. He wanted something short and spiky, the opposite of hippie long hair or cascading prog perms or the androgynous locks of glitter gods. "I really thought all this stuff out in '73 and '74," Hell recalled in the mid '80s. "I wanted the way we looked to be as expressive as the material on the stage, down to what the posters were like."[18] He wanted to invoke youth, rock iconoclasm, and marketability: "The way I remember coming up with the haircut," he said years later, was by asking "what is it about rock &

---

15 Kent (1977b).
16 McNeil and McCain (1996: pp. 168, 170).
17 Veillette (2000).
18 Kozak (1988: p. 58).

roll haircuts that makes them work. Like the Beatles. And my conclusion was that it's grown men more or less wearing haircuts that five-year-olds of their generation wore. What kind of haircut, I thought, did I have when I was five or six?"[19] If Hell's new haircut — a grown-out butch or buzz from the '50s — also resembled the surrealist playwright Antonin Artaud in an asylum, or even the youthful Rimbaud, all the better. In Television's early years critics would compare Verlaine's haircut, cut in longer layers than Hell's and flipped back, to Artaud's look from Dreyer's film *La Passion de Jeanne d'Arc* (1928).[20]

The band's new look may have been an un-look — "as if they rolled out of bed, came in, and played," as Kristal put it[21] — but it still made a theatrical statement. It combined uncivilized street kid with bohemian poet and Bowery bum: a modern take on being old-fashioned, 1950s if not nineteenth-century, suits and loosened ties, clothing torn just so.[22] It referenced the Bowery Boys — a.k.a. the Dead End Kids, the prototypical cinematic New Yawk hoodlums. (Critics had earlier made the same allusion in describing the Dolls' Bowery ethos.[23]) Heroes first of William Wyler's film *Dead End* (1937), the Dead End Kids became the Bowery Boys, protagonists of serial

---

19 Dalton (2001).
20 Wolcott (1976).
21 Kozak (1988: p. 15).
22 Mitchell (2006: p. 39).
23 "Androgyny in Rock" (1973); Kent, (1974b).

shorts that would still have been shown in theaters when Hell and Verlaine were kids. On the other hand Television resembled the bums who lodged upstairs from CBGB's in the Palace Hotel or were sprawled, mornings, against the wall outside the club: downtrodden but still old-school, sometimes in suits, escapees from a Weegee photo. Stillettoes singer Elda Gentile, who dated Hell for a while, thought Television dressed like old men.[24]

Fliers for Television's debut show — along with the advertisement Ork took out in the *Voice* — reinforced their rejection of androgyny: "There was not another rock & roll band in the world with short hair," Hell recalled. "There was not another rock & roll band with torn clothes. Everybody was still wearing glitter and women's clothes. We were these notch-thin, homeless hoodlums, playing really powerful, passionate, aggressive music that was also lyrical."[25] Still, the flier photo walks a finer line between camp and cool than Hell lets on: Verlaine has his head on Hell's bare shoulder, gazing into the distance like a zombie. Hell may or may not be awake behind his shades. Lloyd, in a blond bowl cut, looks away from the camera, and Ficca engages viewers with a coy pout. Though the band disavowed glitter's excesses — no makeup, no women's clothing, no funky-chicken Jagger poses, hands on hip, elbows out — they still looked a little dolled up, in man-drag.

---

24 Harry, et al. (1998: p. 16).
25 McNeil and McCain (1996: p. 172).

The fliers for their debut included a constellation of voices that characterizes the cultural cauldron from which the band emerged. Endorsements came from a range of tastemakers, all associates of Ork's: *Interview* editor Scott Cohen called them "Killers. Sharp as tacks . . . They made me cry." Danny Fields declared: "They're finally here — in full pathological innocence . . . Color, skin, guitars: *Love in Spurts, Eat the Light, Enfant Terrible."* And Nicholas Ray, director of the 1955 James Dean classic *Rebel Without a Cause*, called the band "Four cats with a passion." The cultural blessing from *Interview* suggests a target audience of Max's back-room smart set. As *16's* editor, Fields suggests an almost parodic ambition to become fave raves, top of the pops, though Fields was also well known for his connections to Iggy and the MC5. Nicholas Ray speaks to the significance of the '50s to the transforming underground. His *Rebel Without a Cause*, in punk chronicler Nicholas Rombes's words, offered "a vision of disaffected and alienated youth that is strangely prophetic not only of the Beats, but of other subcultures such as the punks."[26] By 1974, '50s nostalgia was cresting in the mainstream and underground alike: Malcolm McLaren, who the following year would be smitten with Richard Hell's aesthetic, had already opened his London teddy boy boutique, Let It Rock. Back in the states, George Lucas's film *American Graffiti*, with a soundtrack full of fifties jukebox gems, paved the way

---

26 Rombes (2009: p. 231).

Figure 3.1 Television, 1974. L-to-R: Lloyd, Verlaine, Hell, Ficca. Photo by Jay Craven, Copyright Richard Meyers, courtesy of Fales Library, NYU

for Garry Marshall's smash TV series, *Happy Days*, which premiered in January '74.[27]

Television was less interested in television, though, than in the *idea* of television (fig. 3.1). For their inaugural show, 2 March 1974, Ork booked the Townhouse Theater, where Suicide and the Fast had just played and where the Modern Lovers had given a farewell show shortly before that.[28] Located on W. 44th St. at Sixth Avenue, the venue seated fewer than 100 and served as a preview theater for art films, notably Fellini's.[29] The show's stage concept, designed by Hell,

27 Rombes (2009: pp. 88–9).
28 Robbins (2001).
29 Mitchell (2006: pp. 40–1).

played on the band's name and drew on the flavor of '60s Happenings, especially Warhol's Exploding Plastic Inevitable, if more minimally and muted. Hell later recalled: "I had four TV monitors on stage and they were turned on to various channels. We had a guy in the audience roaming around with a portapack video camera shooting live in to one of the TV sets."[30] Though the band never repeated this gimmick, others took notice. Within a few years, after Television had secured its preeminence on the scene, Lou Reed himself would perform backed by TV sets.

No one recalls being satisfied with the show — "we used to fall over a lot on stage,"[31] Lloyd said looking back — but Television's ship had officially launched. Within weeks, perhaps even within days, band members and Ork had met Hilly Kristal and secured a Sunday spot at his newly renamed club on the Bowery.

In 1974, Hilly Kristal was a 43-year-old ex-Marine who had already been in the music business for years as owner of two other clubs — one called Hilly's on West 9th and another Hilly's on 13th. Even earlier he managed the Village Vanguard, where he booked Miles Davis and Nina Simone, Lenny Bruce and Woody Allen. He'd also promoted a Central Park concert series. The Village versions of Hilly's, not far from Reno Sweeney's eventual location, had drawn neighbors' ire for the loud music Hilly booked — some country, some cabaret — and so he turned his attention

---

30 Swirsky (2003).
31 Jones (1977).

to the Bowery. His decision to rename the club CBGB in 1973 may have been a late attempt to cash in on the cowboy vibe the East Village poetry scene had fostered through the '60s: CBGB's featured Wednesday poetry nights for its first two years. The country theme also built on the honky tonk vibe he'd fostered in the Village, where he'd even sponsored hayrides and, on occasion, imported live farm animals. The idea that country might be the next big scene wasn't as far-fetched as it would later seem: country had made a decent showing in 1973 at Max's, with acts like Waylon Jennings, Willie Nelson, Gram Parsons, and Charlie Rich all sharing the same stage that welcomed the New York Dolls. Hilly originally took the idea of "uplifting gormandizers" quite literally, too, planning to spread sawdust on the floor and serve country breakfast to his patrons come sunrise.[32] Still, country music turned out to be only part of the line-up for CBGB's first year; without a consistent line-up of country acts, the club returned to Hilly's earlier eclecticism.

During the club's earlier incarnation, wide-ranging offerings already contained elements that would flow in to punk's formative pool: Hilly's first stage was built by Eric Emerson and Sesu Coleman of the Magic Tramps, the first group to play there.[33] Hilly's also hosted the Bowery Chamber Music Society, the jazz of the Rashied Ali Quintet, and even (after hours) Bette Midler, who was living at the Broadway Central

---

32 Kozak (1988: p. 6).
33 Fletcher (2009: p. 315).

and performed at nearby Hilly's on the Bowery (and more frequently at Hilly's on 9th Street) after long nights as a cast member of Broadway's *Fiddler on the Roof*.[34] Her sets included a cover of the Shangri-Las' "Leader of the Pack,"[35] the bad-girl-group anthem that would later inspire CBGB's acts such as Blondie. In 1971 Hilly's hosted the San Francisco drag troupe the Cockettes, who like Wayne Country later claimed to have kicked off the international glitter and glam scenes. *Voice* critic Robert Christgau, who maintained in 1977 that he was far too old to be a punk,[36] was a regular at Hilly's before it became CBGB's. Later he would tell Roman Kozak that he had one of his first meaningful conversations with his future wife following a Cockettes show there.[37]

Other Hilly's acts that would later appear at CBGB's included Wayne County, who was also a regular at Max's and at Club 82, a venerable drag venue nearby on East 4th Street, where the last of the old-school female impersonators shared their stage with glitter bands. Debbie Harry later remembered the 82 as the destination of choice for New Jersey high schoolers following graduation or the prom,[38] but in the post-Mercer era it had become a primary site for glitter's refugees. The Dolls famously performed there in high

---

34 McCormack (1973).
35 Christgau (1972).
36 Christgau (1977).
37 Kozak (1988: p. 55).
38 Hermes (2007).

drag in April '74; some of the early CB's bands, including Television and the Stillettoes, followed suit; and rock celebrities including Bowie, Reed, Lennon, and the Who were sometimes seen holed up at corner tables.

Wayne County's presence at Hilly's and CBGB's indicates additional continuities between underground theater, glitter, and punk. County had one of downtown's largest cult followings: her early shows at the Mercer and in downtown lofts — some still factory spaces by day, "full of drills and lathe presses"[39] — were typically taken as an extreme version of what the critic Miles, writing in the *International Times* about the Dolls, called "post-Rolling Stones New York faggot rock": "Marc Bolan, Slade, Elton John, David Bowie . . . [combined] with such historical figures as The Fugs, the early Mothers [of Invention] and the very much present day Lou Reed."[40] County tells a slightly different story about transatlantic transgender influence: Her stage career, like Patti Smith's, began in the Theater of the Ridiculous, and she'd traveled to London in '71 with Andy Warhol's play *Pork*, which pushed David Bowie toward new heights of gender-fuck.[41]

In some ways, Wayne County's appearance at Hilly's and CB's suggests the clubs weren't as odd a presence on the Bowery as some later accounts would indicate. The nearby theaters, the legacy of an older vaudeville district, occasionally featured drag

---

39 *Village Voice* writer Richard Nusser, in Kozak (1988: p. 9).
40 Miles (1972).
41 "Bowie Knife" (1995).

shows, but the Bowery had an even longer-standing entertainment culture. In the nineteenth century it had been Broadway's working-class shadow, running from Cooper Square south to the notorious Five Points. The Bowery Theatre, near Canal Street, catered to rowdy antebellum audiences who liked their theater rough and loud; the famed Bowery B'hoys, who would later lend their name — if not its spelling — to the silver screen's Dead End Kids, made the Bowery a fashionable working-class promenade, a stage on which they parodied aristocratic affectations. When the gentry invaded the neighborhood in the 1840s, taking over working-class leisure gardens and erecting a fancy-pants opera house at Astor Place, local butchers and B'hoys rebelled, staging a riot that brought out the National Guard and ended in civilian bloodshed. Half a century later, an estimated 25,000 men lived in Bowery missions and welfare hotels. Through the middle of the twentieth century the Third Avenue El ran along the Bowery, casting a permanent shadow on sidewalks along either side. One result: the Bowery remained the domain of the down-and-out for 150 years. In CB's early days, the walls next to the stage featured oversized portraits of nineteenth-century Bowery burlesquers, an homage to the street's pop cultural legacy.

Hilly's primary clientele in the early '70s was as uneven as the neighborhood's reputation. In addition to some stray drag performers from the Bouwerie Lane across the street, he'd poured drinks mostly for members of the Hell's Angels, whose HQ was nearby, and residents of the Palace and other adjacent flophouses. "I ran it for a while as a derelict bar," Kristal later recalled, "and bums would be lining up at eight in the morning, when I opened the doors."[42] And though the neighborhood had supported upperclass slummers of one sort or another since the middle of the last century, there was nothing mainstream about its appeal. Drivers locked doors when bums offered to wash windows at intersections: in his 1973 novel *Great Jones Street*, about a Dylanesque rock star who holes up downtown to escape his celebrity status, Don DeLillo describes the Bowery as full of these "wild men with rags."[43] Invariably, early press on CBGB's stressed the club's undesirable location. It was a district even cabdrivers avoided, stripped-out cars on the sidestreets and trash-can fires on corners at night. Then again, the kids who came to CB's by and large came on foot. And though "[a]nybody who passed 315 Bowery after ten o'clock in the evening risked getting a knife in the back," as Karen Kristal remembered about the early days,[44] the danger lent street cred to a self-consciously underground movement.

Although Hilly had run *Times* listings using the name CBGB as early as the summer of '73, journalists have traditionally followed his lead in dating the name-change to December of that year. But with the new awning Verlaine and company had see him hang a few

---

42 Kozak (1988: p. 2).
43 DeLillo (1973: p. 159).
44 Kozak (1988: p. 3).

months later, Hilly threw an official grand re-opening in March of '74, only a few weeks before Television's first show there. His opening night, Wednesday the 20th, featured ridiculously cheap drink specials, followed by three nights of the Con-Fullam Band, a bluegrass act from Maine. The next week he advertised three nights of Elly Greenberg's country blues over a smaller, innocuous listing for Sunday: "ROCK Concert TELEVISION March 31." Another ad for the first show, paid for by Ork, foregrounds a photo of the band and also lists the "fancy guitar pickin's [*sic*]" of Erik Frandsen.

Television's first Sunday shows may or may not have attracted enough patrons to allow Hilly to make money from the bar, but they did lead to a confluence of interests and talents that would be significant to Television's — and the scene's — development. Ork, Hell, and Verlaine brought friends from Cinemabilia, including their fellow employee Rob Duprey, who would go on to form Mumps and would later play drums with Iggy Pop. Ork also drew on his Max's connections, and Hell worked literary circles. The biggest payoff came on the third Sunday of Television's residency, when Hell succeeded in getting his friends Patti Smith and Lenny Kaye to drop by and see his new band.

Smith's arrival at the club is clearly the most fortuitous event of Television's and CBGB's early phase — and of her early career as well. Smith has narrated the scene consistently for over three decades: how she knew Hell through the poet Andrew Wylie, whose book Hell had published; how she talked Lenny Kaye into heading downtown to CB's following a press screening of *Ladies and Gentlemen, The Rolling Stones*. Her biographer describes her as arriving in her best Baudelaire: "a boy's back suit, crisp white dress shirt, skinny tie,"[45] but Smith recalls wearing "a black velvet Victorian dress with a white collar."[46] Either way, she was dressed to meet peers who also wanted to bridge poetry and rock. She and Kaye had spent the last few months rehearsing as a trio with a new pianist, Richard Sohl, in order to make an earnest stab at performing as an electric cabaret ensemble, if not quite yet a full-fledged rock act.

When they came to CBGB's to see Television, Smith's group had just come off a five-night, two-sets-per-night run at Reno Sweeney opening for Warhol star Holly Woodlawn. Andy himself had shown up one night; his *Interview* magazine had profiled Smith the previous October.[47] In the spring of '74 Smith was on the rise, turning up in London rock magazines for her relationship with Allen Lanier, to whose Long Island band, Blue Öyster Cult, she'd contributed some lyrics. *Melody Maker* had referred to her as "a poet who appears at New York rock clubs," and Nick Kent in *NME* already dubbed her "the remarkable N.Y. poetess."[48] But it was Television's raw set, together with images of the

---

45 Bockris and Bayley (1999: p. 102).
46 Smith (2010: p. 239).
47 Green (1973).
48 Charlesworth (1974); Kent (1974a).

Stones' 1972 tour in her head, that made her sense something big was about to give. What Smith found, when she arrived on the Bowery in April 1974, would lift her from the outer orbit of the nostalgic cabaret circuit and help to establish her own sense of vocation as a rock star. As Smith would describe it, Television was nothing short of rock 'n' roll Messiahs.

Together Smith and Hell would be Television's and CBGB's earliest and most influential mythologizers, and Smith would outlast Hell as a booster for the band. Ork later told Legs McNeil that Patti had come up to him after her first Television show and said, "I want him. I want Tom Verlaine. He has such an Egon Schiele look."[49] (Schiele's paintings featured lanky, often nude and sexually suggestive figures, who do bear a remarkable similarity to Verlaine's body type.) For the next three years she worked behind the scenes to ensure the success of Television and CBGB's, with all the fervor of a missionary, even as she crafted her own rock poetess persona in full public view.

Television fit right into a narrative Smith had already been crafting in her criticism. Like John the Baptist wandering through the wilderness, she'd both proph-esied and searched the stars for signs of revolution. In the March 1973 issue of *Creem*, Smith called for a "dirtier," more "old school" form of rock than she saw around her; she thought it might be "coming down and we got to be alert to feel it happening. something new

---

49 McNeil and McCain (1996: p. 171).

and totally ecstatic."[50] Her sense of pending revolt may have been influenced by the Dolls, but she seemed less than satisfied with glitter's vaudeville groove. "I really felt that was it, what I was hoping for," she later said of her first time hearing Television: "[T]o see people approach things in a different way with a street ethic but also their full mental faculties."[51] To this day she narrates the moment as portentous: "Tom Verlaine had definitely read *A Season in Hell*," she writes in her 2010 memoir *Just Kids*. "As the band played on you could hear the whack of the pool cue hitting the balls, the saluki [Hilly's dog] barking, bottles clinking, the sounds of a scene emerging. Though no one knew it, the stars were aligning, the angels were calling."[52]

If Smith recognized Television as Ginsbergian "angel-headed hipsters," that revelation was relatively exclusive in 1974. Press on Television's earliest gigs is slim. In April they registered on the radar of the year-old *SoHo Weekly News*, which for the better part of a decade competed with the *Voice* in covering the downtown scene. (Its early distribution plan was to have employees stand outside Max's and hand papers to the crowd at closing time.) Writing about the first string of Sunday shows, Josh Feigenbaum mistakenly refers to the band as Television Set, yet offers valuable insight into their formative stages. Feigenbaum compares them to Hamburg-era Beatles: "disjointed

---

50 Heylin (1993: p. 129), idiosyncratic punctuation in original.
51 Fricke (2007: p. 383).
52 Smith (2010: p. 240).

black leather jacketed and bad," turning out "the kind of music you might hear coming out of some poor bastard's recreation room in suburban Long Island, loud, out of tune and pretentious as hell." If the Dolls hadn't been playing the Bottom Line the same night, Feigenbaum wrote, "the place would have been packed to the rafters." And even though Television had room to grow, their attitude compensated. "[F]or all of their musical ineptness," he wrote, the band

> understand[s] in a basic way what their presentation is about. They sort of exude a nastiness which has always been part of R & R. Through all of their heavy metal histrionics — the great thing about this band is they have absolutely no musical or socially redeeming characteristics and they know it.[53]

Television liked the line so much they used it on fliers and ads for future gigs. It's hard to imagine a more perfect nutshell for what would before long be called punk: do-it-yourself, back-to-basics rock that sloughed off the water-logged carcass corporate rock had become.

A month later Patti Smith's first piece about the band appeared, also in *SoHo Weekly News*. That fall a revision of this piece, suggesting collaboration with band members, would appear in *Rock Scene*, but the original channels her gut reaction and lays out the key elements of the band's mythology. Above all, Smith emphasizes sex appeal: "Confused sexual energy makes young

---

53 Feigenbaum (1974).

guys so desirable," she writes. "Their careless way of dressing; Their strange way of walking; filled with so much longing." She sets the stage, too, by minutely describing CBGB's itself, which she incorrectly locates as "a dark little soho bar" with a "Lousy P.A., long nervous dogs running random, women smoking french cigarettes and mostly boys on the prowl hanging by a thread waiting for Television to tune up."[54]

Smith also repeatedly mentions the band's apparent insanity, another attempt to locate them in Beat or longer Romantic literary traditions. She highlights their cover of "Psychotic Reaction," calls their music "maniac," and quotes some "non-believers" in the audience who suggest they look like "escapees from some mental ward." One early Monday morning following a midnight gig, someone told her they were "just too insane but me," she concludes, "I heard this funny flapping of wings, and the wild boys the wild boys the wild boys . . . just smiled."[55] These last lines reference Burroughs's 1971 novel *The Wild Boys*, on whose protagonist she would later model her character Johnny in the song "Land," just as Television would the eponymous hero of its first single, "Little Johnny Jewel": the unsupervised adolescent male, dangerous and sexual and beautiful, traveling through a violent, apocalyptic landscape. In spite of her rigorous attention to their heterosexual posturing, the final line queers them in her most overt effort to make them

54 Smith (1974a).
55 Smith (1974b).

Romantic outlaws, a tradition inspired not just by Beats but by a form of "antisocial innocence" that Hell, like Smith, derived from Rimbaud.[56]

Television's association with Smith was mutually beneficial. Her cult status turned a spotlight on the band, and especially on Tom, who launched a relationship with her in spite of the fact that she was living with Allen Lanier. Smith's doo wop-inspired "We Three," eventually released on her 1978 album, *Easter*, depicted her simultaneous relationships with both musicians. Its opening lines invoke both CBGB's and Verlaine: "Every Sunday I will go down to the bar / and leave him the guitar," she crooned. He reciprocated with one of his best early songs, "I'm Gonna Find You," a bluesy slow-boiler about a lover with "shiny dirty black hair" and "clothes they just don't make anymore," which transforms into a murderous revenge ballad after she leaves him. Smith's shows were already being reviewed in national publications — *Creem* reviewed one of the Reno Sweeney gigs — and in September she performed with Sam Shepard in a revival of *Cowboy Mouth*. "I started makin' my move when all the rock stars died," she told one interviewer. "Jimi and Janis and Jim Morrison. It just blew my mind, because I'm so hero-oriented. I just felt total loss. And then I realized it was time for me."[57] Verlaine helped give her older poems a rock 'n' roll makeover.

By summer's end, Smith and Verlaine were "definitely a twosome," and had been dubbed, in a gossip

56 Noland (1995: p. 584).
57 Baker (1974).

column Danny Fields had started writing for *SoHo Weekly News*, "the Downtown Couple of the Year thus far."[58] Patti showed up at one show with a bouquet of flowers, marching through the crowd to place them at Verlaine's feet.[59] She and Tom danced to the Who's "Call Me Lightning" on the club's jukebox.[60] When Debbie Harry caught them making out in the alley behind the joint, Verlaine blushed and Patti told her to fuck off. ("But then again, Patti didn't really ever talk to me much," Harry would add, telling the story years later, after Blondie had made it big.[61])

That summer Verlaine helped Smith record her first single, a rendition of the standard "Hey Joe" (prefaced by a poem about the famous kidnap victim and publishing heiress Patty Hearst), backed with her song-poem "Piss Factory," the story of her escape from blue-collar piece work in Jersey, which culminates in her boarding a train for New York, where she plans to become "a big star." Verlaine played a guitar Smith had purchased for him, and they recorded the songs during a three-hour rental at Hendrix's Electric Ladyland Studio. Mapplethorpe bankrolled a thousand copies of the 45. If Patti intended to become a star, she planned to take Verlaine and company with her.

In addition to writing about them, Smith paved the way for an extended co-headline at Max's later that

58 Fields (1996: p. 20 [1 Aug. 1974]).
59 Bockris and Bayley (1999: p. 103).
60 Rader (2009).
61 Bockris and Bayley (1999: p. 104).

year by spending July opening there for Elephant's Memory, Lennon and Ono's sometime backing band. Smith's summer shows at Max's gained the attention of *Times* columnist John Rockwell, who placed her songs "somewhere between Kurt Weill and early Velvet Underground, with their out-of-tune tinny tackiness and their compulsive repertory of three-chord nineteen-fifties riffs." In terms of her "words and ideas," Rockwell pays her a high compliment: Lou Reed, he wrote, isn't even in her league.[62]

Sometime in 1974 Richard Hell sketched out his own review of Television, written from an outsider's perspective. Describing CB's atmosphere first — the smell of dogshit, the "damned dog" itself, the noise of the pool tables, the punch-drunk finale of Music Machine's "Talk Talk" pounding from the jukebox — he eventually turns his attention to the band:

> They were all skinny and had hair as short and dirty and ragged as their shirts. Their pants didn't fit very well but were pretty tight with the exception of one guy who was actually wearing a very baggy 20-year-old suit over his torn shirt. While the lights were still down they continued to tune for five minutes looking intense and sharing a cigarette. The pool table was abandoned and some fancy-looking numbers at the door were trying to talk their way past the $2.00 admission. A little guy with big shoulders in a Hawaiian shirt went over and told them to go back to New Jersey.[63]

---

62 Rockwell (1974).
63 Hell (2001: pp. 39–40).

Hell's one-by-one run-down of the band members begins with Verlaine, "with a face like the Mr. America of skulls," who stands frozen, his mouth moving like a machine to let the lyrics escape. His solos verge on epileptic fits, his "eyes shut like somebody barely able to maintain consciousness." Lloyd stands between Verlaine and Hell, his guitar slung low. He has a "perfect male-whore pretty boy face," Hell writes, "alive with such fear and determination as he wracked the guitar for you could almost hear his mother scolding him. He looked like he was going to cry." Hell himself wears "black boots, the baggy suit, and sunglasses." His hair is short on the sides, spiked on top "like anticipating the electric chair." Hell's antics, like Verlaine's, run to extremes: at first he stands comatose, head lolling, drooling from the corner of his mouth, "and then suddenly [he'd] make some sort of connection and his feet would start James Browning and he'd jump up in the air half-splits and land hopping around utterly nuts with his lips pointed straight out at you." Billy Ficca has his head "held like you tilt your head to tune in on a sound." The band's overall vibe is "raw, perverse, and real as the band members looked." For Hell there is no distance between image and authenticity, though there's serious conflict within the image itself: are these psychotic tough guys, or are they Dickensian orphans? This was the same antisocial innocence Smith had emphasized. "They looked so vulnerable and cold at the same time," Hell writes, "I wondered how they'd lived long enough to get here." The piece concludes: "Me and some other people think they're the best band in the world," then deflates the whole as some kind of maniacal ego trip with a deadpan closer: "Anyway, I went home, started to write a book, and then asked my sister for a blow job."[64]

Hell's voice shines through another account of the band from 1974. Apparently written as a press release, the one-sheet typewritten page fixes specific elements of the Television myth, including Tom and Richard running away from school and being arrested in Alabama before eventually making their way to New York. Tom appears as a child prodigy, misunderstood by his parents, who read "gory" comic books, watched sci-fi flicks, and listened to free jazz before moving on to Absurdist playwrights and the Velvet Underground. Hell was a text-book juvenile delinquent, a "problem child" who "blew up school buses" and listened to only two albums, *The Rolling Stones Now* and *Bringing It All Back Home*. He earned his ticket to New York by working in a porn shop, and after he arrived he "began writing and publishing imitations of decadent French poetry." Lloyd's contribution to Television's mythos came here, as everywhere else, via his hustler persona: "since the age of 17 [he] has fended for himself in New York and Hollywood." He'd also done time in an asylum, something he would later elaborate on in constructing his own public front. "He's probably the most social member of the band," too, "being seen almost every night at an event, a nightspot or a party," and "[l]ike Richard Hell, he likes his glass of liquor." Billy Ficca,

---

64 Hell (2001: pp. 39–40).

in his turn, had started drumming before he owned his first set — another precocious child musician — and joined a band with Tom in Wilmington as a teenager. His cred came from a long line of work: he'd played with "the best Chicago blues band in Philadelphia" and with a Top 40 covers band in Boston. We're told that Ficca is the "most diligent at practice" of the band members and that he spends his spare time screening "B" movies on his huge TV.[65] The press sheet ends by situating Television as East Village locals: Billy and Tom live together on 11th Street and the rest of the band live "in the neighborhood." The gesture — one of belonging — grounds the group in what was now a richly symbolic space. CBGB's was turning into a neighborhood bar for unsigned musicians.

Through the end of '74, "new music" still only made up part of the club's calendar. For the most part, the early CB's rock nights were still hard to separate out from the glitter scene, the Theater of the Ridiculous, or the campier end of the cabaret circuit. The club served food and for the first few years kept booths and tables or folding chairs rather than standing room around the stage. The scene's contiguities with cabaret and glitter are also apparent in Television's choices of other performance venues. In April '74, Television played off-nights from CB's at the Hotel Diplomat's gay discotheque, on one such occasion opening for the local glitter act Dorian

---

65 The press release is reproduced in the unpaginated illustration insert in Heylin (1993). For handwritten drafts of these bios, see Richard Hell Papers, Box 9, Folder 622, undated.

Zero. The Dolls were still stars of the downtown scene, returning from a year of touring in Europe and the U.S. and played two homecoming shows at Max's, followed by a night at Club 82. (This was the show where the band members — with the exception of Johnny Thunders — performed in full drag.) The support act for their New York shows that spring was the Miamis, made up of Wayne County's backing band.

Club 82 soon announced Wednesday night "Live Rock" shows, which competed with CB's poetry nights. A few weeks after the Dolls' big gig at the 82, Television and Leather Secrets — an act that had been opening their shows at CBGB's — played there. Fronted by singer and poet Camille O'Grady, who would later appear in gay art porn and on San Francisco's leather scene, Leather Secrets delivered scatological, proto-punk songs with titles like "Toilet Kiss," often delivered from a gay male persona.[66] At Club 82, Television's audience included David Bowie, who gave the band a line they first used in an ad for a 12 May gig back at CB's: "The most original band I've seen in New York. They've got it."

A week earlier Hell had landed a spot at CB's for the Sillettoes — Debbie Harry, Elda Gentile, Chris Stein, Fred Smith and company — who dished up an homage to the '60s girls group sensation and Queens natives, the Shangri-Las. The Stillettoes had strong ties to Max's, where Debbie Harry had waited tables and where Elda Gentile had been a back-room regular

---

66 Fritscher "Introduction" to "The Academy."

as Eric Emerson's girlfriend. Gentile had a child with Emerson but that spring was seeing Richard Hell. The group's bass player, Fred Smith, would leave the Stillettoes with Stein and Harry to form Blondie that summer; the following spring Smith would make another departure to replace Hell in Television.

As Television honed its sound, the celebrities in Club 82's audiences, Bowie's relocation to New York, and persistent curiosity about the Dolls all returned British press attention to the downtown rock scene. In the summer of '74, on the heels of the Dolls' sophomore album, Chris Charlesworth of *Melody Maker* came sniffing around CBGB's, Club 82, and the Mushroom, a glitter-friendly venue on E. 13th Street where Television would share a bill with the Miamis at the end of June. Charlesworth's two-page spread, which ran in July, depicts an underground still steeped in Mercer's-style theatricality: "Shock and outrage is the name of the game. The more freak-ish, the more outlandish the fetishes of the personnel and the more bizarre their clothes the better. It's not much more than grabbing a guitar, learning a few chords, applying lipstick and bingo!" Charlesworth places Television among others in this late glitter scene: Teenage Lust, the Fast, Jet Black, the Stillettoes, Another Pretty Face, and the Brats. The audience for these bands, especially at Club 82, was composed of "Female impersonators, transvestites and their ilk," with an "element of bisexuality run[ning] strong."[67]

---

67 Gimarc (2005: p. 13 [6 July 1974]).

If the Mercer's Warholian sensibility sustained itself through much of CBGB's first year (on "new music" Sundays anyway) so did the avant-garde theatricality of the downtown arts scene, suggesting that Television's Bowery Boys schtick was just one of several possible costumes acts could don. Alan Vega and Martin Rev's electronic duo, Suicide, had been performing what they called "punk masses" since the fall of 1970. They later claimed to have borrowed the term from Lester Bangs, who used it in *Creem* in December 1970 to describe Iggy Pop, but their fliers include the phrase a month earlier. Suicide appeared at CB's in June of '74 in support of the Fast, a bubble-gum glitter band from Brooklyn who were remaking themselves as mod revivalists.[68] Suicide's punk masses consisted of sometimes violent displays of aggression directed at their instruments — leaving Martin Rev bleeding on occasion — and a threatening posture in relation to the audience, as in Vega's signature move: swinging chains from the stage like a medieval cowboy twirling a lasso.

In mid-August Debbie Harry and Chris Stein played their first show at CBGB's with their new group, Angel and the Snake, soon to be renamed Blondie. Also on the lineup was the Ramones, making their CBGB's debut as well. Both bands typified the new scene's ongoing indebtedness to Warhol as much as they pointed, at this stage, to something new. The Ramones' frontman, Joey Ramone (born Jeff Hyman), had until

---

68 Valentine (2006: p. 78).

that spring sung for the glitter band Sniper under the name Jeff Starship. Tommy Ramone (née Tommy Erdelyi) had toyed with experimental filmmaking and was a sound engineer who had worked with Hendrix and Herbie Hancock. The band also included Johnny Ramone (John Cummings) and Dee Dee Ramone (Doug Colvin), the latter of whom had auditioned to be the Neon Boys' second guitar player a year earlier but hadn't made the grade.

Leather-clad and only acting dumb, the Ramones played up their musical ineptness, something Hell would later claim to have done as well. Like Television, they sloughed off glam trappings and presented themselves as ordinary hoodlums. Initially, at least, some observers saw this as theater. The art critic Dave Hickey wrote in the *Voice* in 1977 that as conceptual art the Ramones were "beautiful." They weren't "just a band," he wrote, but "a real good idea . . . poised with mathematical elegance on the line between pop art and popular schlock. From your aesthete's point of view, the Ramones sound has the ruthless efficiency of a Warhol portrait."[69] Craig Leon, who produced the Ramones' debut in 1976, considered them part of the "the NY underground 'art' scene of The Velvets and Warhol & co.," the world of Patti Smith and Television.[70] The downtown scene-crosser Arthur Russell, a cellist who had worked with Ginsberg and directed the experimental music series at The Kitchen, dragged the composer

---

69 Gendron (2002: p. 256).
70 2004 interview in Rombes (2005: p. 53).

Rhys Chatham to see the Ramones against his will. "While hearing them," Chatham remembered, "I realized that, as a minimalist, I had more in common with this music than I thought."[71] Soon Chatham would begin composing minimalist epics for rock instruments. Though Television was never musically minimalist on the order of the Ramones or Chatham, compared to the excesses of glam, prog, or early metal they were cut to the bone, stripped down. Among the viewers at the Ramones' first show were Alan Vega of Suicide and an art student named David Byrne, who'd just moved into a friend's loft around the corner on Great Jones Street. Vega dug the Ramones' act from the start; Byrne liked them enough that he determined on the spot to form a new band, which he called Talking Heads.

In Joey Ramone's mind the early CB's scene was a seamless extension of period when Hilly's on the Bowery featured the Cockettes, whose members Tomata du Plenty and Gorilla Rose now performed regularly across the street in the "Palm Casino Revue," a drag showcase staged at the Bouwerie Lane Theater. Joey Ramone described his band's earliest CB's audiences as "the Warhol type crowd, like the gay crowd."[72] Dee Dee Ramone recalled that The Ramones' first show at CBGB's in the summer of '74 was "filled with drag queens who had spilled over into CBGB's from the Bowery [*sic*] Lane Theater."[73]

---

71 Lawrence (2009: p. 116).
72 Kozak (1988: pp. 18–19).
73 Ramone (2000: p. 79).

Glitter was alive enough in '74 that Wayne County, Richard Robinson, and others held a panel on the topic for industry insiders that October.[74] KISS's first album had appeared earlier that year; the Queens band had taken original inspiration from the Dolls and other New York glitter acts. But KISS, unlike the Dolls, offered a pronounced distance between their performance on and off stage. The Ramones, like Richard Hell, created characters for themselves that were supposed to break down the barrier between public and private personae. They saw the writing on the Dolls' wall: Johnny Ramone, who had worn spandex and glitter with the best of them, agreed to go with the band's biker jacket look: pre-Ramones, he recalled, "I had on silver lamé pants and a leather jacket with leopard-print fur around the collar. How you gonna get people coming to the shows like that?" It might fly in New York or LA, but they "wanted every kid in middle America to be able to identify."[75] They settled on jeans and T-shirts, sneakers and shades, a more cartoonish version of the look Hell was after. "We were glamorous when we started, almost like a glitter group," Dee Dee later said. "A lot of times Joey would wear rubber clothes and John would wear vinyl clothes or silver pants. We used to look great, but then we fell into the leather-jacket-and-ripped-up-jeans thing. I felt like a slob."[76]

---

74 Fields (1996: p. 21 [10 October 1974]).
75 Leigh (2009: p. 123).
76 Heylin (1993: p. 176).

As the scene continued to snowball, and with a dozen summer performances behind her, Patti Smith co-headlined Max's with Television for ten nights in August and September. "For anybody who cares about What's Happening," Danny Fields wrote in the *SoHo Weekly News*, Smith and Television were "not-to-be-missed, and both of them together makes for the ultimate musical billing of the season, if not the year."[77] Earlier in the summer Fields had raved about "our beloved and fantastic Television," whose show at Club 82 didn't "remind anyone of anything else, because they are so very unique."[78]

Early Television shared with contemporaries like the Ramones a preference for short songs, but they also aimed for a kind of sophisticated engagement with pop music history that set them apart from some of the other downtown bands. One early press release aimed to convey their distinction:

> TOM VERLAINE — guitar, vocals, music, lyrics: Facts unknown. RICHARD HELL — bass, vocals, lyrics: Chip on shoulder. Mama's boy. No personality. Highschool dropout. Mean. RICHARD LLOYD — guitar, vocals: bleach-blond — mental institutions — male prostitute — suicide attempts. BILLY FICCA — drums: Blues bands in Philadelphia. Doesn't talk much. Friendly. TELEVISION's music fulfills the adolescent desire to fuck the girl you never met because you've just been run over by a car. Three minute songs of passion

---

77 Fields (1996: p. 21 [5 Sept. 1974]).
78 Fields, *SoHo Weekly News*, 11 July 1974.

performed by four boys who make James Dean look like Little Nemo. Their sound is made distinctive by Hell's rare Dan Electro bass, one that pops and grunts like no model presently available, and his unique spare patterns. Add to this Richard Lloyd's blitzcrieg chop on his vintage Telecaster and Verlaine's leads alternately psychotic Duane Eddy and Segovia on a ukelele with two strings gone. Verlaine, who uses an old Fender Jazzmaster, when asked about the music said, "I don't know. It tells the story. Like 'The Hunch' by the Robert Charles Quintet or 'Tornado' by Dale Hawkins. Those cats could track it down. I'll tell you the secret."[79]

Another Xeroxed, self-authored press release from the period describes the band as a "peculiarly successful melding of the Velvets, the Beatles, the everly brothers [*sic*], and Kurt Weill."[80] Working out early rough spots on stage, Television gained local notoriety for time spent tuning and for inconsistent performances.

Television also drew attention for its carefully crafted image, especially the torn clothing. On at least one night at Max's, when Television took the stage, Richard Lloyd wore a torn black T-shirt Hell had designed, with the words "Please Kill Me" stenciled in capital letters across the front (fig. 3.2). Though

---

79 Hand-circulated flier, 1974. For a typewritten draft that differs in some details see Richard Hell Papers, Box 9, Folder 594. "The Hunch" was actually recorded by the Bobby Peterson Quintet.

80 Richard Hell Papers, Box 9, Folder 594.

Figure 3.2 Richard Lloyd onstage at Max's Kansas City, 28 August 1974. Photo courtesy of Michael Carlucci Archives

some scenesters would later recall Hell wearing the shirt, he claims he never worked up the nerve. (When Lloyd first wore the shirt at Max's, Hell was wearing a long-sleeved satin shirt with one shoulder torn away.) Lloyd says he volunteered to wear the Please Kill Me shirt only to be deeply unsettled when a few fans at Max's approached him with "this really psychotic look — they looked as deep into my eyes as they possibly could — and said, 'Are you serious?'"[81] If some fans seemed murderous, others seemed suicidal. According to Verlaine, interviewed in early '75,

---

81 McNeil and McCain (1996: p. 173).

There's this group of people that are over forty, ex-suicide types that come up to us after every gig we play, no matter where or how little advertised it was, and they just look like they've seen Jesus. I don't know who they are or where they come from but they're always there, just gaping . . . may be just listening to us is like jumping off a bridge, it's just as good.[82]

This self-conscious, proto-punk nihilism was at the core of early Television songs like "I Don't Care" (later retitled "Careful") or Hell's most popular tune, "Blank Generation." On the latter, Hell updated the chorus of an old Beatsploitation novelty song by Rod McKuen. Instead of singing "I belong to the Beat Generation / I don't let anything trouble my mind / I belong to the Beat generation / and everything's going just fine," Hell offered the wittier: "I belong to the Blank Generation / And I can take it or leave it each time. / Well, I belong to the _____ Generation / And I can take it or leave it each time. / Take it!" On the second run through the chorus the "blank" becomes a moment of silence when Hell withholds the word and the band stops playing, emphasizing the void. As in other Television songs, the song puns elaborately, from the opening line ("I was saying lemme outta here / Before I was even born") to the play on "Take it!" which led directly to Verlaine's solo. The positive impulse to "Take it!" underscores Hell's long-standing argument that by "blank" he intended to convey possibility: "It's the idea that you

---

82 "Television" (1975).

can have the option of making yourself anything you want, filling in the blank," he told Lester Bangs later in the decade.[83] But Bangs and others still read "blank" as abjection; when Malcolm McLaren borrowed Hell's signature style to create the Sex Pistols, he demanded the band rewrite Hell's anthem. Their version was "Pretty Vacant."[84]

Following the Max's gigs, Smith revised her profile of the band for the October *Rock Scene*, in ways that suggest band members' collaborations with her in creating a rapidly consolidating mythology. In the new piece, Smith casts Hell as a "runaway orphan" from Kentucky, "with nothing to look up to." He and Verlaine, she writes, "done time in reform school" before running away. Lloyd "done time in mental wards," a detail that plays on her earlier depiction of the band as borderline insane. ("When I was a little kid, I always wanted to be crazy," Lloyd added at a later date, picking up on the theme.[85]) Billy Ficca, as Smith describes him, had "been 'round the world on his BSA," a real bad-ass. Though most of these elements have some grounding in documentable fact her spin consistently tips toward hyperbole. Despite her insistence that Television "are not theatre" — that they are the antithesis of camp and cabaret — it's clear that their performance is still an act, but one she's willing to buy and to help perpetuate.

---

83 Bangs (1988: p. 266).
84 McNeil and McCain (1996: p. 199).
85 Gholson (1976).

In addition to cultivating the band's mystique, Smith offers here a more mature consideration of the band's relationship to rock history than she had earlier. She recognizes in Television's sound a tension between revolution and revision, between an attempt to break it up and start again, on one hand, and the ways in which these boys inherit the mantle of Chuck Berry, Dylan, the Stones, the Yardbirds, Love, and the Velvets, on the other. Riffing extensively on the band's name, Smith asserts that Television is *real*, unmediated, a point underscored by the fact that they can only be experienced via live shows, not on studio recordings, and that their image is authentic. Smith's difficulty articulating the authenticity/artificiality dynamic in Television's early act suggests an ambivalence toward Warholism that would become more pronounced on the scene over time. "Television will help wipe out media," she declares at one point. Not satisfied with that formulation she expands on it, framing the band as an "original image," something like live television: raw, unpredictable, without rules. Instead of "Hollywood jive," she wants something "shockingly honest. Like when the media was LIVE and Jack Paar would cry and Ernie Kovacs would fart and Cid Cesar would curse and nobody would stop them 'cause the moment was happening it was real. No taped edited crap."[86]

Part of what had been lost for Smith in mainstream rock's studio wizardry and radio-friendly accessibility

---

86 Smith (1974a).

was youthful sexual energy, the thrust of Elvis's pelvis, Jagger's cocky strut, the moves that made early TV execs and some viewers (like her father) uncomfortable. For her, Television's power rested in what she identified as a sort of "high school 1963" sexuality: "Television is all boy," she'd written in the *SoHo Weekly News*, and for *Rock Scene* she elaborates at length. Finding them "inspired enough below the belt to prove that SEX is not dead in rock & roll," she revels in lyrics "as suggestive as a horny boy at the drive in": songs with titles like "Hard On Love," "One on Top of the Other," and "Love Comes in Spurts." She characterizes the band members as variations on a bad boy persona, as if Brando and his gang had just rolled onto the Bowery, set on terrorizing the locals and making off with the nicest of the nice girls. Hell reminds her of *Highway 61*–era Dylan and is "male enough to get ashamed that he writes immaculate poetry"; Lloyd, "the pouty, boyish one," plays "highly sexually aware guitar," "jacks off" on his instrument, even. In her earlier piece she'd identified "confused sexual energy." Though she doesn't say it outright, the implication here is that, unlike the Dolls, these aren't straight kids dressed up like girls or queers. Television "play like they make it with chicks" and "fight for each other" like street kids in a rumble, "so you get the sexy feel of heterosexual alchemy when they play." Verlaine, who "has the most beautiful neck in rock 'n' roll," is a "guy worth losing your virginity to."[87]

---

87 Smith (1974a).

Smith's characterizations play on early Television's paradoxes. They are both highly sexual *and* evocative of virginity or innocence; they are tough guys *and* likely to get beat up by tough guys. Her piece suggests that '50s nostalgia expressed a desire for a pre-Vietnam conflict America, but also a desire for adolescent regression, a return to the pleasures and dangers of being a teenager. Part of what she taps into resonates with with *Grease* on Broadway, or the ubiquity of the Fonz. But she also identifies something larger than mainstream America's simplistic '50s revival. Here, just as punk is starting to stir, she pinpoints what will be one of its most fundamental characteristics, moving across the range of sounds and styles that will be classified as punk in decades to come: Above all else, punks will be "[r]elentless adolescents." She invokes the prototypical Bowery Boys to nail down the point: Television are latter-day "Dead end kids." When Smith comes to the end of this piece, she replaces the collective emphasis on rock seraphim with a vision of Verlaine as a singular "junkie angel." She points to "the outline of his hips in his pants," and then imagines that "he's naked as a snake," Adam and Satan all in one.[88]

Of the just more than two dozen nights Television played in 1974, only nine of those dates were at CBGB's, fewer shows than they played in August and September at Max's with Patti Smith's group. When Fields wrapped up the year for *SoHo Weekly News*, the Max's appearances with Patti received his nod for local

---

88 Smith (1974a).

show of the year. Between that run's conclusion and the end of November, Television hunkered down to rehearse, hoping to follow Smith's example and cut an independent single. CB's plowed ahead without them, maintaining its bluegrass credentials; in between some new music shows featuring the Ramones, the club played host repeatedly to a group called the Hencackle String Band.

When Television re-emerged, it was amidst buzz that record companies were interested in signing them. Fields, announcing that the band would be playing at Club 82 on November 20th and the Truck and Warehouse Theater on E. 4th Street two days later, told his readers to expect "all new songs, and plane-loads of record execs from England, where [Village record store owner] Bleecker Bob has been spreading the word about the mightiest of bands."[89]

The Truck and Warehouse show on 22 November was co-billed with the Ramones, who had gained a fast following.[90] For some reason, though, the Ramones canceled, and Blondie took the stage as opening act, Debbie Harry wearing shades and a silver construction helmet. "We're not the Ramones," she announced. Their set that night included a cover of Television's "Venus de Milo." One audience member recalled

---

89 Fields (1996: p. 22 [14 Nov. 1974]).
90 According to CBGB.com, the Ramones played a staggering 74 performances, or 37 nights, at CBGB's between 16 August and the end of the year. Concert listings and ads in *SoHo Weekly News* suggest that number is hugely inflated.

Lloyd sauntering on stage in the black Please Kill Me shirt. Then "[w]ild-eyed Verlaine announced their first number: 'We're gonna start off with a little ride,' and the boys lunged into a frenzied rendition of the 13th Floor Elevators' 'Fire Engine,' so incendiary I feared the Truck and Warehouse might burst into flames."[91]

Slightly less star-struck was Island Records A&R man and *Melody Maker* columnist Richard Williams — if not quite the "planefuls" of record execs Fields had predicted, still a very important one. Williams had early on, in *Melody Maker*, helped to bring the Velvets to the attention of UK audiences. He had also helped Roxy Music land its first recording contract. At Island he was busily gathering a vibrant stable of avant-rockers, including John Cale, Nico, and Brian Eno. Lisa and Richard Robinson were confident that Television would make a perfect arrow for Island's quiver and escorted Williams to the venue. Recalling the Truck and Warehouse show years later, Williams said "Blondie could barely function" the night he saw them, but he wanted Television to cut a demo for Island straightaway.[92] He even suggested that Eno, prince of London's underground, should fly in to help him cut the tracks. Though Verlaine later suggested that he had little idea who Eno was, that seems hard to imagine: Eno had gained international name-recognition for his work with Roxy Music, which had ended the previous year with him being squeezed out of the band. At the

---

91 Rader (2009).
92 Heylin (2007: p. 26).

start of '74 he'd released his first solo album, *Here Come the Warm Jets*, and he'd just worked on John Cale's latest LP, *Fear*, both on Island. That summer Eno, Cale, and Nico had recorded a concert album for the label. "[T]he playing was awfully rickety, almost amateurish," Williams recalled of Television, "but there was something interesting happening, and most of it was vested in the gawky, angular, pained figure of Verlaine."[93]

That sense of a narrowing spotlight didn't bode well for Richard Hell.

93 Heylin (1993: p. 121).

4

Down in the Scuzz with the Heavy Cult Figures

There were elements of New York Dolls, Warholian elements, a lot of fifties Beat poetry elements, but [with Television] for the first time I was reacting to it as a rock 'n' roll show, as opposed to a be-in, a happening.

— *Leee Black Childers, 1988, in Savage,*
England's Dreaming Tapes *(2010)*

No one talked — ever — about the stock market. No one went to the gym. Everyone smoked. Bands did two sets a night. Television jammed for hours at a time. Onstage (and off), Patti could talk like nobody's business. . . . Patti Smith and Television and the Ramones and Talking Heads and Blondie were like our own little black-and-white 8-mm. movies that we thought would conquer the world.

— *Lisa Robinson*, Vanity Fair, *November 2002*

Television is doing what the Stones would be doing if they were still alive.

— *Joel Sloman*, Creem

Television's so-called "Eno demos" are as fundamental to the band's legend as the story of stumbling onto CBGB's. At the time, the brush with Island Records hinted that Television would be the band to blow the lid off the local scene, to go where even the Velvets hadn't and bring New York's underground into the mainstream. In hindsight, though, the situation also called to the fore creative differences that were emerging between Verlaine and Hell and would result in the latter's departure from the band that April. Listening to the Island demos today, we can recognize a band that was on the road to *Marquee Moon*, but one still struggling to pull itself free of influences and downtown predecessors, even as Verlaine also struggled to undo some of the image Hell had so carefully conceived.

Television's early sets, by most accounts, contained about a 70-30 percent split between Verlaine's songs and Hell's. But following the gigs at Max's in the fall of 1974 Verlaine started pulling Hell's songs from the set lists. At some point the shifting dynamics within the band spilled into the stage set-up as well. Blondie's Chris Stein recalled:

> I liked Television with Richard. With Hell I thought they were fantastic. . . . [Richard] used to do this Townshend thing, a whole series of leaps and bounds around the stage. It was more dynamic. Verlaine was on the end and

> Lloyd was in the middle. Then all of a sudden Verlaine
> was in the middle and it changed things.[1]

Hell's sense that Verlaine was taking control of the band was reinforced by three days near the end of '74 at Good Vibrations, a Latin-oriented studio that hoped to make salsa the "New York sound" of the '70s.[2] Of the six songs they recorded, only "a lame version" of Blank Generation represented Hell's output.[3] The others, all Verlaine numbers, would show up on *Marquee Moon*, with the exception of "Double Exposure," one of their catchiest early songs, though one most showing the Dolls' influence. Of the other tracks recorded with Eno, two were among Verlaine's earliest ("Venus de Milo" and "Marquee Moon") and two were relatively recent compositions ("Prove It" and "Friction"). All but the version of "Blank Generation" would later turn up as the first five tracks of the *Double Exposure* bootleg LP (1992), which also contained a set of demos recorded later that year at Smith's midtown rehearsal space.

Before sessions started, Verlaine had been keen to work with Eno, who was the same age as Television's principals but had already seen substantial success. He was also keen to make a play for an Island contract. The sessions quickly turned sour, though. To Williams and Eno, Verlaine fretted as if the band were laying

---

1 Heylin (1993: p. 121). Fliers for the Truck and Warehouse show feature a photo with Lloyd in the middle.
2 Dove (1974).
3 Swirsky (2003).

down masters, not demos, eager to get the exact sound he wanted. Complicating matters, the engineer, who came with the studio and apparently had more experience with salsa than rock, "couldn't get the hang of the group at all," Williams said years later.[4] Eno, meanwhile, had picked up on the band's indebtedness to '60s garage — there are strong Count Five overtones on these tracks, *5D*-era Byrds, too, if only in the guitars — but Verlaine thought the references came off as too literal, more like the twangy surf-rock instrumentals of the Ventures.

To a number the Good Vibrations tracks do refer more overtly to older rock styles than the later versions on *Marquee Moon* would. "Prove It" contained clever nods to the Latin vibes of early Brill Building girl groups. "Double Exposure" could have been a Dolls cover. "Marquee Moon" hinted at off-kilter reggae in its opening line and a piano part banging below the chorus harkened to the Velvets' repetitive open fifths. Verlaine's vocals, too, are still riddled with echoes of Johansen's snarl or Wayne County's pout. If the arrangements overall are punchier than the versions on *Marquee Moon*, driven by the washtub-thump of Hell's bass, the songs don't yet have the polish or expansiveness they'd develop over the next eighteen months. Still, the session documents mind-boggling advances over material recorded in Ork's loft mere months earlier, and despite Verlaine's displeasure with the sound, Williams and Eno both thought the band

---

4 Heylin (2007: p. 26).

was ready to sign. *Andy Warhol's Interview* did as well, offering the band a brief blurb set next to a gorgeous close-up of Hell and Verlaine: "Eno just produced a *very* high priced demo tape for Island Records who are frothing to sign them up, but till now they've been Manhattan's most closely guarded secret. They have a large cult following who wear ripped clothing like Verlaine and Hell and flock to their concerts."[5]

Richard Williams imagined they might even move to London, as Hendrix had. But much to his disappointment, Island didn't bite. Eno also pitched them to his label, EG, but didn't get any better response. Other versions of the story suggest that Verlaine just didn't like the tapes and called the whole thing off, even though Williams was well on his way to making the demos into an album.[6] By mid-January, word had leaked to Fields: "It's a shock," he wrote, "but Television has apparently rejected a bid from Eno and Island Records for a producing/recording deal."[7] Verlaine told *SoHo Weekly News* that spring that he'd found Eno "an interesting guy, but we just had different ideas of where our music was going."[8] A couple years later he told *Melody Maker* that Eno's "ideas were incompatible with mine."[9] They would be better suited, apparently, to David Byrne, whose band Eno would produce in a few years' time.

---

5 "Television" (1975).
6 "Tom Verlaine" (1995).
7 Fields (1996: p. 23 [16 January 1975]).
8 Betrock (1975b).
9 Jones (1977).

Fast on the heels of the aborted Island demos, Television staged a full-force homecoming on the Bowery, playing their first shows there since the previous July: "TELEVISION RETURNS to CBGB's," trumpeted ads in the *Voice*. During January and February Television played over a dozen dates, two sets a night, usually in three-night runs. Kristal's new "three night policy" would make the club an effective incubator for new acts.[10] Over six sets, bands refined material and drew crowds by word of mouth. Blondie opened Television's January dates. Another half dozen shows in February and March were opened by newcomers Mumps, led by Lance Loud, a proto–reality TV star of PBS's "An American Family," who had come out to his Santa Barbara parents on camera. Influenced by the Dolls and drawn to New York by Warhol, Mumps initially belonged to the glitter crowd. Loud carried on a highly publicized affair with Warhol star Jackie Curtis. Within a few months, their drummer, Jay Dee Daugherty, would be whisked away by the Patti Smith Group.[11]

For most of the past year, CBGB's had welcomed underground rock on Sundays only. Even at the start of '75 the Wednesday to Saturday early slots were held by a Celtic folk rock band called British Misfortunes, and the Wednesday late slot continued as a poetry night. In the new year, however, the underground was coming to

---

10 Charlesworth (1976).
11 Hoffmann, Mumps History; Fields, *SoHo Weekly News*, 7 Nov. 1974.

define the identity of the venue, and vice versa. At the end of 1974, when Ruskin closed Max's for financial reasons, CB's gained a corner on downtown rock. Alan Betrock, writing in the *SoHo Weekly News*, heralded Television's reappearance as a resurrection.

Betrock's account of one January show serves as a referendum on Television's development and on the general scene, giving us a good idea of how things were shaping up down at the club. The selections on the CB's jukebox — a mix of British invasion, disco, glam, R&B, and psych (the Who, the Hues Corporation, Bowie, and Gladys Knight all coexist, somehow, with 13th Floor Elevators) — anticipates his description of the crowd's mélange of "styles and leanings." Blondie's spirited opening set, which included covers of Tina Turner and the Shangri-Las, added to the heady stew of influences. But "the people came to see Television," Betrock notes, "and they did not go home disappointed." Having tightened their sound since they last played CB's, they now "perform a powerfully hypnotizing brand of music" and have amassed "an endless number of classic originals, including 'Venus de Milo,' 'Love Comes in Spurts,' and the much requested 'Double Exposure.'"[12]

Betrock comments on Verlaine, Lloyd, and Hell, finding the latter "most riveting" on "Blank Generation." Picking up on the sexual energy Patti Smith had identified the previous year, Betrock celebrates the way their "pent-up energy . . . spurts out

12 Betrock (1975c).

in their music," especially when songs like "Hard On Love" build to a "masterful climax." Significantly, though, Betrock positions Television as post-glam but doesn't specify the nature of their departures from the earlier scene: "When groups like the Dolls, Harlots, and Teenage Lust failed to create much success after huge advance publicity, most people assumed the NYC scene to be dead. But Television, along with such varied units as Patti Smith, Milk 'n Cookies, and the Dictators prove that New York is alive and well, and predictions of widespread adulation do not seem premature."[13]

Television's local stature was confirmed when they played three shows in March at a new drag venue, the Little Hippodrome, opening for the Dolls, who hoped to stage a comeback under Malcolm McLaren's management. The Dolls had already played three shows there a week earlier (including a Sunday all-ages matinee "for our high school friends") and were generating buzz with a new gimmick in which they wore red patent leather in homage to Red China. Television's three nights with the Dolls were strained by the cold war between Verlaine and Hell. Even so, two weeks later, on the 23rd, the band launched a seven-week scene-exploding stand at CBGB's with the Patti Smith Group, whose manager had teamed up with Ork to convince Kristal that the unprecedented run would boost CB's visibility. Playing two shows a night, four nights a week for seven weeks gave both bands the chance to solidify their stage show and gave Patti's

13 Betrock (1975c).

group a chance to gel with a new five-piece lineup that now included a second guitarist, Ivan Kral, lately of Blondie. As Lenny Kaye recalled these shows: "The experience of playing night after night at CB's kind of hardened us, so that when we played for Clive [Davis of Arista Records] we sounded tight."[14]

The spring residency with Patti Smith built on groundwork laid over the previous year and the buzz Smith had generated for half a decade. Patti's profile was even higher than it had been the previous fall. On New Year's Eve she participated in a poetry extravaganza at St. Mark's, reading alongside Yoko Ono, Allen Ginsberg, and John Giorno. A new show at the Guggenheim included Brice Marden's painting "Star (For Patti Smith)," which placed Smith in a pantheon of musicians for whom Marden had created work, including Baez, Dylan, and Joplin. In February she'd recorded demos for RCA but by the end of March, just as the shows with Television were getting underway at CBGB's, Fields reported that Smith was on the verge of signing with Arista. (Still, he wanted to know, "why are the labels so slow in grabbing Television? Everybody raves about how great the Velvet Underground was, and here is another great New York band that musically picks up where the Velvet Underground left off."[15])

---

14 Kozak (1988: p. 39). Despite Kaye's recollection, Smith signed her contract with Arista only a few days into the spring residency.

15 Fields (1996: pp. 24–5 [27 March 1975]).

Patti's contract arrived at the end of March; John Rockwell announced it in the *Times* on the 28th, only a day after Fields had hinted it was on the horizon and only three days into the run with Television. Davis signed Smith to Arista, the label he'd founded the prior year, offering her $750,000 for seven albums. She would have full creative control, producer's rights, and even a hand in the advertising. Rockwell's piece gave both Television and CBGB's their first notices in the *Times*: "Anyone who wants to see Miss Smith in the ambience in which she has heretofore flourished — the seedy little club — had better hurry on down," he wrote, noting Television as "an interesting Velvet Underground offshoot."[16] The Velvets comparisons came from all quarters. Fields reported two weeks later, rather cheekily, that Lou Reed, having just returned from a two-month tour of Europe, "wasted no time in checking out Television at CBGB, after he read somewhere" — meaning in one of Fields's own previous columns — "that they had picked up where the Velvets left off. Lou, of course, was also anxious to hear his dear friend Patti Smith, and was seen grinning paternally as she performed his song, 'We're Gonna Have a Real Good Time Together.'" In the same column Fields added that "the real big record executives are just starting to get interested" in Television, "judging from who was [at CB's] last weekend, and who is expected this one. It is about time."[17]

---

16 Rockwell (1975b).
17 Fields (1996: p. 25 [10 April 1975]).

Less than a month later, the New York Dolls called it quits. Rockwell fretted in the *Times* about the effects of overexposure on young New York bands. Though he doesn't name groups other than the Dolls and the Velvets, coming as his comments do during the last week of Smith and Television's reign at CBGB's they seem to ask what impact Smith's contract will have on the new scene.[18] And yet Rockwell was complicit as part of the press machine that had been tracking Patti for years — and which she'd explicitly courted. From the moment he broke news of her contract with Arista, the crowds at CB's started to grow until the club was past capacity. "CB's was the first time we had played so many times in a row," Smith's manager, Jane Friedman, recalled a decade later. "We didn't just pack CB's, we had people literally standing around the block who couldn't get in."[19] Fields corroborates: On 17 April he wrote that "Hundreds were turned away from Patti Smith's gig at CBGB last weekend. Way to go, Patti!" At the conclusion of this run, Ork cornered Hilly and told him he couldn't beat these receipts "with your country and bluegrass, dude!" He recalled in *Please Kill Me*: "I considered that the official beginning of the scene."[20]

In early April, as the CB's shows were gaining momentum in the wake of Smith's contract, *SoHo Weekly News* ran a "Know Your New York Bands" piece by Betrock profiling

---

18 Rockwell (1975a).
19 Kozak (1988).
20 McNeil and McCain (1996: p. 172).

Television. The piece pinpoints tensions that would soon lead Hell out of the band and would eventually separate Television from the scene it had helped to establish. Treating Verlaine as the band's clear leader, Betrock gives nods to Hell for "Blank Generation" and Lloyd for "What I Heard," though it's clear these are token turns in the spotlight. Meanwhile, Betrock quotes Verlaine praising Patti Smith but dismissing the general CB's scene as "campy and non-sincere — and that's not the way rock should be."[21]

Though Betrock didn't seem to anticipate that Hell would actually leave the band, Fields caught wind, and in his 10 April column warned "a certain musician in a certain hot new band! Don't leave the group! Wait a year and a half — then you'll be able to do anything you want!"[22] The advice obviously didn't take: the following week Fields reported that in "a shockeroo move, bassist Richard Hell has left Television, to start a new group (details must wait until next week). Replacing Richard temporarily will probably be the bass player of Blondie, and no doubt Television will continue to thrive, but Richard will be missed."[23] The following week he reported on the Dolls' breakup and the formation of the Heartbreakers with Hell and ex-Dolls Johnny Thunders and Jerry Nolan.

Verlaine told the crowd at Television's first post-Hell show, on 17 April, that Fred Smith had

21 Betrock (1975b).
22 Fields, *SoHo Weekly News*, 10 April 1975.
23 Fields, *SoHo Weekly News*, 17 April 1975.

learned 15 songs in two days. Smith later said that he already knew the band's songs fairly well, given a year of performing in opening slots for them with the Stillettoes, Angel and the Snake, and Blondie. On some accounts, Verlaine had been discussing the personnel change with Smith even in advance of Hell's departure; Verlaine even admitted having jammed with Smith on off hours just to feel out the fit.[24] Still others suggest Verlaine had also sounded out Ernie Brooks, bassist for the Modern Lovers.[25] Hell halted production on poetry chapbooks by Verlaine and Smith his Dot Books imprint had planned to publish. Verlaine's *28TH Century*, already typeset, remains unpublished.[26]

Fred Smith had been with Debbie Harry and Chris Stein in one band or another for over two years. In *Please Kill Me*, Harry responds to Smith's departure from the other side of Blondie's breakthrough: "Fred Smith fucking quit Blondie. I was pissed. I was pissed at all of them — all of Television, all of the Patti Smith Group, and Patti and Fred. I was pissed at Patti because she talked Fred into joining Television. Boy, did he make a mistake. Ha ha ha."[27] Photographer Roberta Bayley, who worked the CB's door and was living with Hell at the time he quit Television, also noted the irony that Blondie eventually outstripped Television commercially: "But at that

---

24 Heylin (1993: p. 138).
25 Mitchell (2006: p. 58).
26 Richard Hell Papers, Box 9, Folder 594.
27 McNeil and McCain (1996: p. 196).

point Television was the one tipped for big, big success. Blondie was the worst band in the city — they were just a joke. Everybody liked them personally but they didn't really have it together on a musical level."[28] Patti had already poached Kral from Blondie and Dougherty from Mumps. For Harry and Stein, these personnel shifts marked the end of CBGB's communal era. With Patti's contract a done deal and rumors afloat of others, knives came out.[29] For years Harry would complain that Patti Smith had had it out for her from the start: "Basically she told me that there wasn't room for two women in the CBGB's scene and that I should leave the business 'cause I didn't stand a chance against her! She was going to be the star, and I wasn't."[30]

For many fans, Hell's departure marked the end of an era as much as had the arrival of gawkers, wannabes, and record labels. The acrimonious split intensified over the next two years, especially during the UK media frenzy that followed *Marquee Moon*'s release. Hell and Verlaine's mutual rage seemed evidence of abiding feelings: "[T]he two new wave culture heroes regularly vilify one another with Romeo/Juliet intensity," Vivien Goldman wrote in 1977.[31] Certainly the scenario echoed other high profile falling-outs: Lennon and McCartney, Zappa and Beefheart, Reed and Cale, Ferry and Eno. "It's very hard to know just how honest

---

28 Heylin (1993: p. 160).
29 See esp. Heylin (1993: pp. 160–1).
30 Bockris and Bayley (1999: p. 112).
31 Goldman (1977).

I should be about the reasons for my demise from Roxy," Eno had told Nick Kent in the summer of '73. "The problem is that when it gets printed, it all seems to look much more meaningful and serious when unqualified by that chuckle at the back of the throat. . . . People who do great hatchet-jobs on the members of their old band usually come out looking like losers when it all appears in print."[32]

Kent should have relayed that warning when he started tracking Television in 1976. Instead he helped widen the gulf between the former friends. Kent returned to the states in the spring of '76 to cover the British glam band Sweet at an Ohio gig. Stopping over and returning via New York, on Malcolm McLaren's advice he looked up Richard Hell, hoping to score heroin, and wound up crashing a few weeks on Hell's couch in a perpetual nod. After publishing Hell's side of the break-up that year, Kent offered an ecstatic review of *Marquee Moon* in early 1977, followed only a few weeks later by an article repeating some of Hell's most damning (and most frequently reprinted) characterizations of Verlaine: "I knew though from the very beginning — with Tom — that it'd probably end that way," Kent quotes Hell as saying. "Years and years ago, when we were dropping acid together — God, it'd get very, very scary. He'd really open up then and he more or less revealed that he had this fundamental belief in his absolute inherent superiority to everyone else on this earth."[33]

---

32 Kent (1973a).
33 Kent (1977b).

Kent gave space to this swipe in what was supposed to be a post-album feature on Verlaine, even as he acknowledges Verlaine's dissatisfaction with Kent's earlier piece on the friends' breakup:

> When the subject of Hell occurs in our interview Verlaine has well established a striking propensity for resolute eloquence. He is very concerned about expressing his interests accurately and having them reported exactly as such.
>
> Yes, he'd read my previous NY City article and yes, he was "Rather upset" by the Hell accusations.
>
> "Patti too."
>
> (Verlaine didn't have to remind me of his sweetheart's reactions as I'd spent a taxing half-hour the previous year debating the charges against the lovely Tom with a fraught and very feisty Miss S.)
>
> "I was going to ask *you* about Hell," Verlaine retorts with a slick smirk of sorts on his lips.
>
> So I tell him straight. Hell thinks you're a hot talent — particularly as a guitar-player — but as a human being, he mmm . . . hates you. (Is that it, Richard?)
>
> "Oh, come on now. He doesn't *hate* me, whatever he may say. Let's face it, man, when two best friends sort of go separate ways . . . when that bond is severed, then both parties usually discover feelings about each other that are based on hurt, on aspects of rejection that often manifest themselves openly in very juvenile ways.
>
> "And that's not a slight on him. I was probably as bad."[34]

---

34 Kent (1977b).

Offended by this piece, Verlaine responded by attacking Kent to another magazine's interviewer: "Nick Kent is the guy who prints hearsay, total hearsay," he told the British underground paper *ZigZag* in June of '77. He'd given a platform to Hell, "a guy who's said a million times that he's out to get me, and who'll say anything that's going to make me look bad." No stopping there:

> I don't have any respect for Nick Kent as a person. Anybody that prints gossip about somebody, and then sees them and still prints gossip . . . I mean, I did everything I could to straighten out that stuff, I spent an hour talking to him, and it still came out as . . . he's sick. He gets this fantasy idea about somebody and won't let go, even if you confront him face-to-face about it.

About Hell, Verlaine stepped it up, denouncing him not just as a bad bass player but also as a junkie:

> Let me tell you what happened . . . and I really hope you print this. When Richard Hell left the band he was doing all kinds of heavy drugs, and at that same time Nick Kent was in New York and moved in with him for a couple of weeks. Richard at that time was super-bitter about any involvements he'd had with me, and he totally broke off our friendship. I didn't have anything against him when he left the band. I was still willing to spend time with him, because I like the guy a lot . . . he's my best friend. But all of a sudden there was no communication. Then Terry Ork told me that this guy was living with Richard . . . and he never came over to talk to me.

So whatever Richard told him is, like, all this garbage that came out of bitterness.[35]

There's more here than just "he said/he said" between former friends. The Hell/Verlaine split has been taken to indicate tensions running through the entire scene. The critic Bernard Gendron, for instance, reads this conflict as competing discourses — art versus pop — with Verlaine representing high-minded art aspirations and Hell representing punk's DIY ethos and pop image-orientation. On the larger scene, Gendron argues, art rockers like Talking Heads lined up with Television and Patti Smith, while the Ramones sided with the "fuck art, let's rock" agenda of Hell and his later bands, the Heartbreakers and Voidoids.[36] But this view, though compelling, overlooks ways in which the Ramones and Blondie (and the Dolls before them) grew out of Pop contexts (not just pop, lower-case p); Hell's very image for Television betrays Warholian influence. Plus, part of Hell and Verlaine's beef seems to have resulted from Verlaine's desire for broad commercially viability. Contra Gendron, what emerged during CBGB's first phase was nearly the inverse of his art/pop dynamic, one that aligns art *and* pop bands like Patti Smith Group, Television, Talking Heads, Blondie, and the Ramones with aspirations for commercial success and left other bands — the Voidoids, the Dead Boys — more closely identified

---

35 Kendall (1977).
36 Gendron (2002: pp. 252–4).

with transatlantic punk, which kept an emphasis on the original impulse to stick it to the record industry. Though some believed that punk had commercial potential in the late '70s, its mass appeal would remain much more limited than would the art-pop new wave stylings of Blondie or Talking Heads.

Fred Smith's arrival was to Television what Lloyd's had been to the erstwhile Neon Boys. Things fell into place. The band's sound tightened, taking on a more streamlined tone. Like Verlaine and Ficca, Smith had played in bands throughout high school. A Forest Hills, Queens, native, he'd joined a short-lived band called Captain Video in 1971 and had responded to Elda Gentile's ad for a bass player a few years later, which led him to the Stillettoes. Photos of Fred with the Stillettoes show him in full flash mode: knee boots, velvet shirts, long hair parted down the middle and feathered, eye shadow and lipstick.[37] Fred's bass playing was certainly more fluid and jazz-derived than Hell's, a better fit with Verlaine's impulse to improvise on long, rollicking numbers like "Breakin In My Heart," which shared ground with Patti Smith's improvisatory style. "At the first rehearsal me and Lloyd [were] looking at each other and thinking, 'God, this is a real relief.' It was like having a lightning rod you could spark around. Something was there that wasn't there before. Fred could follow stuff. I remember starting up in the longer songs and being able to do stuff that wouldn't

---

37 See, for example, Bangs (1980: p. 17); Harry, et al. (1998 [1982], p. 18).

throw everybody."[38] Though such comments emerged from the drawn-out feud with Hell, and so should be taken with a grain of salt, Smith's arrival — and the elimination of Hell's material and stage presence — pushed Television toward *Marquee Moon*'s emphasis on precision over rough proximity, even as many fans mourned the loss of Hell's energy on stage.

After 20 nights with Patti, and still weathering Hell's departure, Television played three more four-night stands at CBGB's through June, each with a week or two off in between, headlining over the Modern Lovers as well as newcomers like Planets and the Shirts. In early June, between Television's runs, Talking Heads made their CBGB's debut opening for the Ramones. By now CB's was drawing a couple hundred people per night. But problems seemed to loom on the horizon. In May, Betrock reported a crowd of around 150 for Marbles and the Ramones on a Monday "new band night," including members of several other bands: "2 Televisions; 3 Milk 'n' Cookies; 2 Mumps; 1 Planets; 2 Blondies; 2 ex-Dolls; 1 ex-Television, and so on," along with friends, relatives, hangers-on, scenemakers, and the press. Fretting that only a third of the crowd may have paid admission, Betrock worried that the scene wouldn't be able to sustain itself.[39]

Other tensions threatened the scene's stability. In the wake of the Television/Patti Smith run and the rise of the Ramones, glitter was becoming increasingly

38 Heylin (1993: p. 139).
39 Betrock (1975a).

marginal at CB's, to the degree that one writer, reviewing the previous weekend's "gay erotic poetry rock" of Emilio Cubeiro, warned of a "precarious sex stance" increasingly inhospitable to women and gays. "[T]he musician-dominated C.B.G.B. crowd," this critic worried, was wary of threats to "their heterosexual superiority (and usually sexist) bag." Characterizing the crowd as "young city rednecks" bristling with "teenage machismo," he reported that some audience members were heckling "faggots" to get off the stage.[40] With the Dolls' demise, glitter's wane seemed inevitable. Another blow fell in May, when Eric Emerson was killed by a hit and run driver while biking near the West Side Highway.

The end of the glitter era seemed to be confirmed by the UK press' first major report on CBGB's. The *NME*, which had mentioned Television the previous summer in a feature on the post-Mercer scene, sent 24-year-old Charles Shaar Murray to gauge the local effects of Patti Smith's signing. (Murray, along with Nick Kent, was part of an effort on *NME*'s behalf to tap into new music markets and to attract younger readers.) The report was hardly flattering, yet homed in on a major shift that had taken place over the course of the previous year: "scuz" had replaced "flash," Murray announced. "C.B.G.B. is a toilet. An impossibly scuzzy little club buried somewhere in the sections of the Village that the cab-drivers don't like to drive through." The scene that had sprung up there

---

40 Baker (1975).

featured "chopped-down, hard-edged, no-bullshit rock 'n' roll, totally eschewing the preening Mickey-Mouse decadence that poleaxed the previous new wave of N.Y. bands." Television provided one of his chief examples of the new order, since they "don't dress up and they don't even move much."[41]

Anticipating a key descriptor of punk in the coming years, Murray frames Television as "an imaginative return to [rock's] basics." He also sees them as "a total product of New York," a blend of the "traditional and the revolutionary." Verlaine, he writes, "was evidently severely traumatized by Lou Reed at an impressionable age" and performs "frozen-faced and zombie-eyed, alternately clutch[ing] his mic stand with both hands and blaz[ing] away at off-balance methedrine speed-fingers lead guitar marathons." Lloyd features as "spraddle-legged and blank-eyed, chopping at his Telecaster like some deranged piece of machinery, braced so that he can lurch in any direction without falling over. He's wearing Fillmore East T-shirt, which is the ultimate in dressing down." The bass player (it's not clear if he'd seen Smith or Hell) "wears his shades on every other number." The common thread is a detachment from the audience more characteristic of the new movement than its predecessors, though one that had clear precedent in the coolness modeled by Dylan and Lou Reed. "That a band like Television are currently happening and that people are listening to them," he wrote, "is indisputable proof that rock

---

41 Murray (1975a).

is a hardier beast than much of the more depressing evidence would suggest."[42]

The transatlantic seal of approval seemed to validate and vitalize the scene: Fields gushed in the *News* about Murray's "raving" review of Television and Patti Smith: "I'll bet he had been expecting to hate" Television, Fields said, noting that the band had "attract[ed] international attention without yet having signed a recording contract."[43] Finally recognized on their own terms — and not just as afterthoughts to the Velvets or the Dolls — underground bands also edged their way into mainstream domestic publications that summer. Lisa Robinson, now a champion of the Ramones as well as Television, followed a *Rock Scene* feature called "Ballroom on the Bowery" with a more substantial scene profile in *Hit Parader*.[44] That summer the *Voice*'s music editor, Robert Christgau, declared Television the "most interesting of New York's underground rock bands," and noted that Fred Smith's arrival led "aficionados" to identify a "thicker" sound in recent shows.

Some uncertainty remained about the final effect of Hell's departure. Offering the most perceptive criticism of the band to see print since Patti Smith's early mythmaking, the *Voice* writer Richard Mortifoglio zeroed in on Verlaine's stage-presence and Hell's absence. The more animated Verlaine became in recent shows, the more "spittle and sweat flew off his

42 Murray (1975a).
43 Fields (1996: p. 26 [12 June 1975]).
44 Heylin (1993: p. 182).

mouth as he screamed," he couldn't escape his own reticence, Mortifoglio wrote, which was his "most affecting and engaging quality." There's some irony that the focus here, in the wake of Hell's departure, trains on Verlaine's image more than on the music. But Mortifoglio sees in Verlaine's "austere personal style" a "graceful self-effacement" that lends to Television's mystique, the projection of a "Gary Cooper man-child, stunned into an electric metaphor by the shock of city life." The recurrence of electric metaphors in Verlaine's lyrics, poetry, and stage presence suggested the "ecstatic insanity" of his own self-invention: "like a village idiot visited by tongues, [he] suddenly become articulate enough to communicate exactly how it is up there." Ficca and Lloyd seem to distract from Verlaine's transcendent effect, Mortifoglio feels, and not even Smith's "cushiony undercurrent," which newly grounds Television's songs, can make up for the "conceptual void" Hell left behind. In spite of technical shortcomings, Hell had balanced Verlaine's "mystifications" through his "wide-eyed loony tunes." Now Verlaine just seemed lonely. Hell, that is, would continue to shape Television's image even in his absence, which served to make Verlaine, the "genuine auteur," all the more "precious."[45]

In the summer of '75, CB's crackled with electricity, notwithstanding the feeling some old-timers had that its clubhouse days were past. A whole bohemian genealogy now materialized on the Bowery like

---

45 Mortifoglio (1975).

ghosts inhabiting descendents' homes: Ginsberg and Burroughs could be seen at tables near the stage. Lou Reed now regularly hung out. "[A]ll those types of people," one regular would recall, "which [lent] an underground poet-beat sort of feeling to it."[46] At the end of June Bob Dylan resurfaced in the Village, making an impromptu appearance at a show Patti Smith played at the Other End (as the Bitter End was briefly renamed) on 26 June. When he introduced himself afterwards, the press heralded the meeting of old and new scenes and treated Patti like a star. "He said to me, 'Any poets around here?'" Patti reported, "[a]nd I said, 'I don't like poetry anymore. Poetry sucks!' I really acted like a jerk." When photographers approached them backstage, she pushed Dylan aside and said: "Fuck you, take *my* picture, boys!"[47] On 7 July their photo showed up on the *Voice*'s cover with the headline: "Tarantula Meets Mustang: Bob Dylan Gives His Blessing to Patti Smith." Dylan played several shows in the Village that week as part of the First Annual Village Folk Festival, including sets with Muddy Waters and Ramblin' Jack Elliott. On the 12th he showed up with Bobby Neuwirth, Patti Smith, and Tom Verlaine in tow. Patti, described by one less-sympathetic *Voice* reporter as "your basic androgynous Keith Richard freak" — joined Dylan on stage for several numbers while Verlaine watched

---

46 Photographer Maureen Nelly, in Heylin (1993: p. 237).
47 Bockris and Bayley (1999: p. 122).

from the audience.[48] Before long Television would add Dylan and Stones songs — "Knockin' on Heaven's Door" and "Satisfaction" — to their setlists, usually as encores.

Two weeks later Television hit the road to Ohio for their first out-of-town gigs. Patti had sequestered herself in advance of recording her debut album with John Cale. CBGB's, meanwhile, was held down by Talking Heads and the Ramones. The invitation to play Cleveland's Piccadilly Inn came from Peter Laughner, a *Creem* writer and member of the Cleveland-based Rocket from the Tombs. Laughner had been to New York that summer and was transformed by seeing Television play. In Cleveland, Laughner's band opened for Television both nights, though the New Yorkers rolled into town just as Rocket was imploding. (Its members would later resurface in punk bands Pere Ubu and Dead Boys, both of which would make strong showings in New York.) Television, for its part, played two respectable sets, soldiering through old standards ("Hard On Love" "Poor Circulation") and newer ones (a rousing version of "Foxhole," in which the suggestive opening line "*Hey*, soldier boy!" is replaced by a more antagonistic shout). They also displayed their new tendency to improvise, with gradually expanding versions of "Little Johnny Jewel," "Marquee Moon," and a rocking ten-minute rendition of "Breaking In My Heart," which departed from a Velvets-like

---

48 Shelton (1986: p. 447); Leichtling (1975). During the '70s Richards omitted the "s" from his surname.

"White Light White Heat" stomp to proceeded along Patti Smith's spoken-word line, gradually bringing a chattering crowd to silence. Laughner had built up Television to mythic status among the Cleveland scene, with only a tape of four live tracks to support his case. As his bandmate Cheetah Chrome (later of Dead Boys) would recall years later, Laughner wanted Television all to himself, exacerbating tensions within his own band. Verlaine, Chrome recalled, seemed unapproachable, distant.[49]

According to Fields's column in the *News* on 24 July, several of Television's New York fans made their way to Cleveland for the concerts.[50] A few weeks later Laughner raved about their live sets in *Creem*, more national press for a band that still hadn't signed a recording contract:

> No, they don't have a record out yet, and they'll probably be hard to translate fully onto vinyl (records don't have eyes like Tom Verlaine), but these people play with the tactile intensity of those who've looked hard and long at things they could never have. "Fire Engine" and "Breaking In My Heart" are as good as anything the Velvet Underground ever cut, and since it's 1975, maybe much better.

Rock Scene ran photos of the Cleveland shows several months later, in January '76, under the headline "Television Visits the New Liverpool."

49 Chrome (2010: p. 127).
50 Fields (1996: p. 27 [24 July 1975]).

When the band returned to New York, CBGB's had already been the site of an underground rock festival for two weeks — what Kristal was billing as a showcase for "New York's top 40 unsigned bands." Targeting summer weeks when nothing much was happening downtown, Hilly had no problem finding bands to audition despite the stifling heat. He turned acts and patrons away. The initial ads, for shows running from July 16 to 27, listed 24 bands in alphabetical order: "Antenna, Blondy [*sic*], City Lights, Day Old Bread, David Patrick Kelly, the Demons, Jelly Roll, Johnny's Dance Band, Mad Brook, Mantis, Marbles, Movies, Mink DeVille, Planet Daze, Ramones, Raquel, Shirts, Silent Partners, Sting Rays, Talking Heads, Television, Tuff Darts, Trilogy, and Uncle Son."[51] Short sets started late and ran through the night, winding down at four or five o'clock the next morning. Crowds spilled onto the sidewalk outside the club. The "Arabian swelter," James Wolcott wrote in the *Voice*, was exacerbated by a broken AC system.[52] Along with Wolcott, other local press supporters swung into action. The *Voice* listed the festival as a pick, though it warned, defensively, that the club's atmosphere wasn't as exotic as *NME* had made out. Hell and Thunders's Heartbreakers headlined the second weekend, the same nights Television was playing Cleveland. Although Television was named in the early ads, they only returned in time to play the final

51 Kozak (1988: p. 42).
52 Wolcott (1975a).

two nights of what was already a substantial extension, headlining over Marbles, Talking Heads, and the old Mercer's act Ruby and the Rednecks on Saturday and Sunday, August 2–3. Crowning CBGB's highest profile event yet, Television reigned as undisputed kings of the unsigned underground.

Post-festival press was substantial and aimed to make Big Statements about the meaning of what the September *Rock Scene* dubbed the "New York IMPLOSION!" Writing in the *Voice*, Wolcott called the festival "the most important event in New York rock since the Velvet Underground played the Balloon Farm" and identified what he saw as a "conservative impulse" in the new wave, by which he meant a back-to-basics "counterthrust to the prevailing baroque theatricality" of corporate rock. But Wolcott stresses that CB's isn't a "flash" scene like the Mercer: regulars are "dressed in denims and loose-fitting shirts — sartorial-style courtesy of Canal Jeans." New bands heralded a retrenchment: they would call mainstream rock's dinosaurs — the Who, the Stones, the Beach Boys — back to edgier '60s roots. It's no accident, Wolcott writes, that 1975's album of the year so far was "a collection of basement tapes made in 1967."[53]

Wolcott celebrates CBGB's above all as a place that allowed bands to refine their sounds in front of live audiences. Television offers his prime example of the fruits of this approach:

---

53 Wolcott (1975a).

[T]he first time I saw them, everything was wrong — the vocals were too raw, the guitar-work was relentlessly bad, the drummer wouldn't leave his cymbals alone. They were lousy all right but their lousiness had a forceful dissonance reminiscent of the Stones' "Exile in Main Street," and clearly Tom Verlaine was a force to be reckoned with.

He has frequently been compared to Lou Reed in the Velvet days, but he most reminds me of Keith Richard. The blood-drained bone-weary Keith on stage at Madison Square Garden is the perfect symbol for Rock '75, not playing at his best, sometimes not even playing competently, but rocking swaying back and forth as if the night might be his last and it's better to stand than fall. Though Jagger is dangerously close to becoming Maria Callas, Keith, with his lanky grace and obsidian-eyed menace, is the perpetual outsider . . .

Tom Verlaine occupies the same dreamy realm, like Keith he's pale and aloof. He seems lost in a forest of silence and he says about performing that "if I'm thinking up there, I'm not having a good night." Only recently has the band's technique been up to Verlaine's reveries and their set at the CBGB festival was the best I've ever seen: dramatic, tense, tender . . . with Verlaine in solid voice and the band playing *as a band* and not as four individuals with instruments. Verlaine once told me that one of the best things about the Beatles was the way they could shout out harmonies and make them sound intimate, and that's what Television had that night: loud intimacy.[54]

---

54 Wolcott (1975a).

Wolcott's piece, elevating an unsigned local band to comparison with the biggest band in the world, is significant for its careful consideration of the new scene's relationship to its predecessors, whether British invasion, Mercer's glitter, or the amphetamine-fueled Happenings of the Exploding Plastic Inevitable. Unlike '60s Happenings, though, which aimed for total involvement of the spectators (Wolcott quotes John Cale on this point), the new bands aimed for cool detachment. And as for the holdovers from glitter, Wolcott wants none of them: he doesn't mince words in dismissing Ruby and the Rednecks and lobs a grenade at their supporters in the *Interview* crowd. The Ramones, by contrast, Wolcott thinks are a "killer band." Obviously, for him they have shed any early Warhol overtones.[55]

That fall, Television decided to follow Patti Smith's example and release an independent single. Smith was now in the studio with John Cale recording *Horses*, where Verlaine played guitar on "Break It Up," a song he'd co-written. He continued to see Smith romantically, though she was still entangled with Lanier, who also appears on the LP. With Smith's career moving into high gear, it was time for Television to make its move. Recording at Patti Smith's midtown rehearsal space, with each band member in a separate room, they used a four-track Teac tape deck into which Verlaine plugged his guitar directly, with no amplification. The band recorded six songs, most of which had been on

---

55 Wolcott (1975a).

the Picadilly Inn setlists: "Hard On Love," "Careful," "Friction," "Prove It," "Little Johnny Jewel," and "Fire Engine." Notably absent, considering they were thinking about a single, was "Venus de Milo," which as one of their oldest crowd pleasers would have been a natural choice.

Some of the arrangements from the fall '75 demos suggest the band's trajectory toward increased accessibility. "Hard On Love" (which shares a title with a Marc Bolan record from '72), for instance, has been slowed to a gentler Latin beat, with pleasant arpeggios in the lead guitar line and a comforting call-and-response in the chorus (Verlaine sings: "You're so hard on love" and the band responds: "Tell me why, tell me why"). But Verlaine seized on the most inaccessible of these tracks as his choice for the single: "Little Johnny Jewel," a seven-minute song that epitomized his tendency toward visionary Romanticism. Think William Blake, Verlaine told a reporter for *Crawdaddy!* some months later: "He was the same kinda guy." The song stages a conflict, then, between Romanticism and modernity: "Johnnie [*sic*] Jewel is how people were maybe two hundred years ago," Verlaine went on to explain:

> Back then, when people got up in the morning, they knew what they had to do to get through the day — there were 100% less decisions. Nowadays, we have to decide what we want to buy in grocery stores, what job to take, what work to do. But not Johnnie. For him,

it's all right there — it's a freer state, and that's what my music is looking for."[56]

The song follows Johnny, who's somnambulistic or perhaps stoned, to an airfield, where, "with a chest full of lights," he crouches behind a fence while airplanes roar overhead, taking off and landing. It takes minutes to narrate this sequence before Johnny "loses his senses" and Verlaine's guitar, spasmodically approximating Johnny's derangement, itself takes into flight, the solo climbing higher and higher as Lloyd strums a rhythm line that recalls Link Wray's "Rumble" (1958). Verlaine jams for two and a half more minutes — Nick Kent would later disparagingly, though with uncanny accuracy, compare the solo to Country Joe and the Fish — before the band coordinates a come-down and Verlaine reprises the opening lines. "If you see him looking lost," the song advises in its finale, "You don't got to come on so boss." Come on in what sense? Is Johnny Jewel, like the character in the Ramones' "53rd and 3rd," turning tricks? Perhaps: "All you gotta do for that guy / Is wink your eye." Others have suggested that Johnny's prototype may have been Verlaine's twin brother, John, whose heroin addiction would eventually claim his life in the mid '80s.[57] In any case, if Kent is right that the song recalls Barry Melton's proto-psych guitar solos with Country Joe and the Fish, it's as if the guy in that band's "Not So Sweet Martha

56 Elliott (1977).
57 Mitchell (2006: ch. 12).

Lorraine" actually *was* in the city, trying to get back in the subway of Martha's mind. As the roaring engines of "Little Johnny Jewel" made clear, Television's music has no patience for country life, period.

The Blakean reference suggests that Johnny is more than a simple observer of modernity. He's prophetic, "Just trying to tell a vision." Like Blake's, Verlaine's own poetry had been preoccupied with vision, violence, flashes of lightning, and sensory doubling — what Ginsberg called "Blake-light tragedy" — meant to suggest the capacity for, and yet the tendency to fall short of, transcendental experience. In a 12-minute live version from 1978, released in 2003 on *Live at the Old Waldorf*, Johnny is stymied not only by modernity's predilection for "preferences" but also by the drudgery of day labor on the docks: "Pick it up there, and put it over there," he's told, over and over and over, until he finally flees in order to find himself the recipient of revelation near the runway.

"Little Johnny Jewel" recalls Patti Smith's sense of Television as a band both Messianic and vulnerable. Written in the wake of Hell's departure from the band, its boy-hero with lights in his chest echoes an image Hell had developed in an unpublished novella, *The Voidoid*, written around the time the Neon Boys folded but unpublished until 1996. Hell's story featured characters loosely based on Verlaine and Hell — Skull and Lips — and included a long sequence narrated from the Hoboken hooker-poet Theresa Stern's point of view. The image from the novella that resonates with "Little Johnny Jewel" involves Hell's avatar, Lips, a vampire who develops a hole in his chest, which eventually fills with a bulb, then a lens, then a television for a heart: "The hole in there gets a picture, and he thinks, 'Maybe this is what the hole is for?'"[58] The image would return in an article Hell wrote about the Ramones for *Hit Parader* after he'd left Television: "The music The Ramones create from [their general frustration] is incredibly exciting. It gives you the same sort of feeling you might derive from savagely kicking in your smoothly running TV set and then finding real thousand dollar bills inside."[59] If the vampire had grown a TV heart, a few years later that heart had shattered.

Verlaine's choice of "Little Johnny Jewel" as the band's first single created a major conflict. By far the longest track they had recorded, it clocked in at just over seven minutes and would have to be spread over both sides of a 7-inch single. "Careful" or "Fire Engine" would have been closer to a three-minute radio edit and either would have made a more accessible vinyl debut, as would have the catchier "Hard On Love" or "Prove It." Lloyd thought Verlaine's choice was disastrous. The song wasn't yet well known by fans of their live shows, and it didn't pack the punch of their steady-building double boilers, such as "Marquee Moon" (equally problematic given the length: so much so that they didn't even record it at this juncture). The solo belonged entirely to Verlaine. Plus, there would

---

58 Hell (1996: p. 50).
59 Hell (2001: p. 41).

be no B-side, hence no exposure for another song. Verlaine would later say he had conceived it more as an album than as a single.[60]

In Verlaine's defense, however, this problem wasn't exactly unprecedented in American rock: Dylan's "Like a Rolling Stone," itself six minutes long in willful disregard of radio formats, had been spread over two sides of a 45 rpm disc, at least on the promotional versions given to DJs. "[T]he other side was just a continuation," Dylan had explained in a press conference at the time. "[I]f anyone was interested they could just turn it over and listen to what really happens."[61] Verlaine may have had similar feelings about "what really happens" in the second half of this song. Alan Licht notes how radical Verlaine's move was: "[F]ew bands of the day would have thought of documenting themselves for art's sake using a medium that was mainly geared toward radio play."[62]

Lloyd threatened to quit if Verlaine went ahead with his choice, and that's exactly what happened. The single, underwritten by Terry Ork, launched the Ork label. Less than ten days after the tracks were recorded, Fields reported in his 28 August column that Lloyd had left the band, to be replaced by "a famous musician from Cleveland." For several weeks it looked as if Peter Laughner really would join Television, especially after Fields reported that Lloyd would launch a new band of

---

60 Verlaine (1976).
61 Marcus (2005: p. 3).
62 Licht (2003).

his own. In October the single went on sale at Village Oldies, by mail order (advertised in the *Voice* and in *Creem*), and at the door at CBGB's. Despite Lloyd's reservations, the *Voice* gave it prominent notice in its centerfold spread:

> A SMOKING 45: "Television," one of New York's best underground bands, has released a single, "Little Johnny Jewel (Parts I and II)," which is characteristically dynamic and spooky — Tom Verlaine sings as if a knife were being held to his throat. The record doesn't capture Verlaine's Texas-chainsaw intensity (his live performances are *thick* with tension) but its dissolute aura isn't easy to shake off.[63]

The same issue that featured this rave from Wolcott also included an ad for shows Television was slated to play at Mother's with a UK band called Bananas. Wolcott's concert listing notes that fliers for the show, posted around downtown, announce Tom Verlaine rather than Television: in any case, Wolcott felt, this would be a "should-see event": "Verlaine and crew are erratic in performance but their material is unique, and when they rise to the moment, they're thrillingly out of control."

Before the Mother's shows could take place, peace was somehow brokered between Verlaine and Lloyd. Laughner was dismissed. He returned to Cleveland where he wrote a wistful review of the single for *Creem*:

---

63 Wolcott (1975b).

Live, in person, where your eyes and your groin and your undercover Sigmund Freud connections to the realistics of rock 'n' roll can all be engaged at once, Television put out the kind of energy and mania that must have permeated the Marquee Club on Who nights circa 66. Trying to describe TV in print has sent rock-print luminaries like James Wolcott & Lisa Robinson scurrying to their thesauruses for words like "dissolute" and "chiaroscuro." Trying to play with each other has caused Tom Verlaine and his various partners (one of whom for a week was me) all kinds of hypertense fall-down-the-stairs scenes but brother, IT WILL STAND!

This is the best band in America right now, it's like a subway ride thru a pinball game, like coming and puking at the same time, and they don't sound like the Velvets and they don't sound like Stooges, THEY DON'T EVEN SOUND LIKE NEW YORK BANDS ARE THOUGHT TO SOUND . . . and problematically enough, they don't sound AT ALL like this single. But you should buy it, the least of reasons being that someday you will have it to show to yourself and your friends and say "See . . ."[64]

Some listeners, hearing Television for the first time on vinyl, were as enthusiastic as Laughner. In London, Vic Goddard, who would soon help form the British punk band Subway Sect, had imagined Television would sound like something else entirely as he stared at New York gig posters Malcolm McLaren prominently displayed in his new fashion boutique. When he eventually heard the single, he "thought it was a modern

---

64 Laughner (1976).

jazz quartet. I was totally blown away — it was one of the best things I had ever heard."[65] Others, especially those who favored the band's earlier incarnation with Hell, were perplexed or put off. Charles Shaar Murray, returning to New York to profile the "Sound of '75," called it "rotten." *Creem*'s lead critic, Lester Bangs, agreed. Both would turn out to be short sighted, as the single would become a collector's item and the song a crowd favorite. The 15-minute version performed in 1978 and released on the bootleg cassette *The Blow Up* (1982) would be compared by Christgau to Coltrane; the solo, he wrote in the liner notes, was Verlaine's "ultimate statement."

The shows at Mother's in October '75 featured Television in its mature incarnation, having weathered a close call with another personnel change that may have proven disastrous, given the band's increasing reliance on the interplay between its two guitarists as one of its defining elements. Set lists now included a new song, the funereal, Oriental-chainsawed "Torn Curtain," which would appear on *Marquee Moon*. "Marquee Moon," now an audience favorite, was clocking in at over eight minutes, the dueling guitar solos now sounding like the braided bolts of lightning referenced in the lyrics. (The song's climax and dénouement, though, remained to be evened out.) Wolcott, writing in early 1977, recalled one of the Mother's shows as the moment Television's "image came in crisp and clear." He shared a table with Richard Robinson, Lou

---

65 Heylin (2007: p. 75).

Reed, and Reed's current flame, a Club 82 drag queen named Rachel:

> [T]hroughout the evening Lou grumbled and bitched about everything and nothing, like a sailor with a sore case of the clap. When Television did its version of Dylan's "Knockin' On Heaven's Door," Lou finally made a grouchy exit, but some loose voltage of rancor hung in the air, and when TV concluded with its anthem "Kingdom Come," the song surged with angry force. Towards the end of the song, Verlaine broke a string, then methodically broke every string, snapping them with stern malicious delight; he then laid his guitar down, and went to his amplifier and began slamming it against the wall, slamming it hard and obsessively, with the manic cool of Steve McQueen assaulting a pillbox in "Hell Is For Heroes." The band kept playing, Verlaine kept pummeling the amplifier, and, finally, Verlaine abandoned the battered amplifier and sauntered off stage and the kingdom come was spent.[66]

This wasn't the first time Verlaine had engaged in this sort of assault on his equipment. Back in July, Richard Mortifoglio had described a very similar act of "strangely quiet violence," shortly following Hell's departure from the band, when Verlaine "ripped all the strings off his guitar and them methodically knocked his amp around a bit." Instead of nodding to McQueen's portrait of a soldier on a suicide mission, Wolcott should have recognized Verlaine's act as an echo of

---

66 Wolcott (1977).

Jeff Beck's assault on an amplifier in Michaelangelo Antonioni's 1966 film *Blow-Up*, itself modeled on Pete Townshend's infamous guitar-smashing antics. In the film, pieces of Beck's guitar pass from the stage into the audience like a sacrament, starting a riot while the Yardbirds chug through "Stroll On." In Verlaine's case, too, smashing equipment seemed liturgical, a ritual by which he let band members go or took them back, in either case for the sake of the music. He was, you could say, just trying to tell a vision.

5

Punk Is Coming

The [CBGB's] bands weren't really alike. There was a self-awareness to their work that spoke of some knowledge of conceptual art — these weren't cultural babes-in-the-woods, despite Johnny's and Joey's and Dee Dee's and Tommy's matching leather jackets. Tom Verlaine once said that each grouping was like a separate idea, inhabiting their own world and reference points. Of them all, I loved watching Television grow the best.

> — *Lenny Kaye, intro to*
> Blank Generation Revisited, *(1996)*

Patti Smith's *Horses* appeared in November to general acclaim and brisk early sales. Lester Bangs, in a rave review for *Creem*, declared she was backed by "the finest garage band sound yet in the Seventies" and discerned in her songs a heady mix of "the Shangri-Las and other Sixties girl groups, as well as Jim Morrison, Lotte Lenya, Anisette of Savage Rose, Velvet Underground, beatniks, and Arabs."[1] The *New York Times Magazine* profiled her in December, though the

---

1 Bangs (1976).

piece had nothing on the rest of the downtown scene and instead featured a photograph of her with Dylan. At the end of December her band played three nights at the Bottom Line for a star-studded audience that included Hollywood actors, most of CBGB's major players, rising rock luminaries such as Springsteen and Peter Wolf (with his wife, Faye Dunaway), and the rock critical establishment, including Jann Wenner, *Rolling Stone*'s editor, who had been slow to come around to the new New York sound. Television joined Smith's band on stage at least one night, as did John Cale. "[S]imply, it was a wonderful weekend," wrote Danny Fields, "and it bodes well for everyone involved."[2]

As 1976 began, Television seemed ready to fulfill that promise. The sound that would make *Marquee Moon* was more or less in place. Once they began performing new compositions "See No Evil" and "Guiding Light" in late '75, all the songs were written that would eventually be on the album. Their live shows attracted larger crowds than ever: at CBGB's they broke house records two nights in a row in December before headlining the final show of CB's Christmas Rock Festival on New Year's Eve. Smith joined them on stage at CBGB's around 5 am to help them finish their second set. Fields, who named Television and the Ramones the "Cosmic Newcomers" in his year-in-review column, reported that Lou Reed had been won over as a fan, that the underground film director John Waters had been to see them, and that Paul Simon

---

2 Fields (1996: pp. 29–30 [1 January 1976]).

had come to a show in November with Arista's Clive Davis.[3] But still no contract, a situation that would wear thin Television's relations to other CB's bands over the coming months, as Verlaine came to feel more and more distant from the scene he had helped start. Some of their peers — starting with the Ramones — had negotiated contracts of their own. He would feel even more separated from the musicians overseas who would form the UK punk scene, many of them fueled by legends of New York's Bowery enclave.

When the *NME* sent Murray back to New York near year's end to find "The Sound of '75," he somehow missed Television's live shows. He did hear the single, though, which couldn't live up to his memory of seeing the band live the previous spring, and so he only offered the band a mixed review in his feature, which was the most extensive the scene had received overseas. Noting the band's "wilful inconsistency," he concedes: "And since they still haven't recorded anything impressive (viz the debacle of the Eno Tape, a tale of almost legendary status in CBGB annals), it seems unlikely that any of the major labels who've decided that they can get along without Television are likely to change their minds unless a particularly hip A&R man manages to catch Tom Verlaine and his henchmen on a flamingly good night."[4]

That a reporter from the *NME* was talking about

---

3 Fields, *SoHo Weekly News*, 30 October, 27 November, and 25 December 1975.
4 Murray (1975b).

having heard the "legendary" Eno tapes seriously unsettled Verlaine. It's not quite clear when Verlaine first heard Roxy Music's new album *Siren*, but by the end of '76 he was telling reporters he believed Richard Williams or Brian Eno had distributed their demo tape so promiscuously that Ferry had ripped off at least a dozen lines. Roxy's song "Whirlwind," for instance, included the line "This case is closed," Verlaine's sign-off in "Prove It." But Verlaine's list of resemblances seems superficial. The lack of a contract seemed to be pushing him toward paranoia. As early as December '75, Danny Fields had noted Lou Reed's habit of taping CBGB's shows on a portable Sony cassette recorder, still a novelty.[5] But when Reed packed his recorder into a Television show in the summer of '76, Verlaine bristled. Lisa Robinson took notes on the confrontation, which came on the cusp of Television's finally signing with Elektra:

> "What's he doing with that tape recorder?" mumbled Tom Verlaine. "Do you think I should ask him to keep it in the back?" Ask him for the cassette, I suggested, or the batteries. "Hey, buddy," Verlaine said to Reed. "Watcha doin' with that machine?" Lou looked up, surprised. "The batteries are run-down," he said. "Oh yeah?" responded Verlaine. "Then you won't mind if I take it and hold it in the back, will ya?" Lou handed a cassette over, then said, "You'd make a lousy detective, man. You didn't even notice the two extra cassettes in my pocket, heh-heh." Verlaine was not amused. "O.K. then,

---

5 Fields (1996: p. 29 [18 December 1975]).

pal, let me have the machine. I'll keep it in the back for you." Reed handed over the machine, then said, "Can you believe him?" His eyes widened in surprise.[6]

Verlaine's paranoia may have been warranted: when Reed played the Palladium at the end of '76 in support of his *Rock and Roll Heart* LP, he played in front of a bank of Television sets, as if to stage a pissing contest with the new underground.

As 1976 began critics still grappled with how to label the music on the downtown scene. A profile piece by Lisa Robinson in *Creem* called the CB's bands the "new Velvet Underground." John Rockwell, in the *Times*, continued to use the label "underground rock," and in January he placed Television at the top of the "pecking order [that] has emerged on the feverishly active New York" scene. Talking Heads, whom he personally found more "gripping" than Television, followed close behind.[7] The search for a label flexible enough to accommodate the broad-ranging CB's scene ended in the first weeks of the year, when fliers popped up around the neighborhood announcing that "PUNK Is Coming." They heralded the arrival of a new magazine, whose first issue appeared in January, obviously influenced by *MAD*, hand-lettered and with a Frankensteinish Lou Reed on the cover. The image simultaneously suggested Reed's repeated return from the dead and also the way the new scene had

---

6 Robinson (2002).
7 Rockwell (1976a).

been stitched together from ingredients including large chunks of the Velvets' corpse. "DEATH TO DISCO SHIT!" thundered John Holmstrom's first editorial headline. In *Punk*'s second issue, a supposedly drunken Verlaine dispenses a dissertation on the French poet Gérard de Nerval (he preferred Nerval to Paul Verlaine), and Richard Lloyd suggests that "you can't admire life unless you admire death." *Punk* asks Television's guitarists about their historic stint at CBGB's with Patti. "We were playing there a year and a half before we did that," says Verlaine, a tad defensively. Lloyd chimes in: "Two years." Verlaine: "But nobody knows that. At least two years." Lloyd mistakenly asserts it was April or May of '72, and Tom offers a version of the origin myth in which he and Lloyd discover the bar. When *Punk* asks about Theresa Stern's *Wanna Go Out?*, Tom answers: "Teresa's in the hospital. Yeah. She had a breakdown . . . in Hoboken. She was turnin' on some John and she — she just — her mind just snapped. I don't think she writes no more. She's the Syd Barrett of the poetic scene."[8] Over time it would become clear that *Punk*'s editors preferred the straight-forward pummeling of the Ramones or the raw intensity of Richard Hell's bands to Television's more cerebral anthems: "party punk" over "arty punk," in terms Wolcott would later use.[9]

In February yet another new magazine appeared on the scene: *New York Rocker*, edited by *SoHo Weekly*

---

8 *"Punk* Talks" (1976).
9 Wolcott (1996: p. 74).

News's Alan Betrock, with staff writers including Debbie Harry, Roberta Bayley, and Theresa Stern (now a solo pseudonym for Hell), who offers a humorous review of a Heartbreakers show. Like *Rock Scene*, *New York Rocker* helped create the sense that local culture heroes were already stars — "before they'd even crossed the Hudson," as the magazine's second editor, Andy Schwartz, recalls.[10] Much more than *Punk* did, *New York Rocker* lavished attention on Television (fig. 5.1). The debut issue featured Verlaine on the cover and, in its centerfold, included an extensive autobiographical sketch, in which he described his childhood music experiences on piano and sax, his twin brother ("I believe that stuff about twins having this ethereal connection between each other"), his high school friendship with Hell and their experience running away, his introduction to Genet and Kerouac. The extensive space devoted to this narrative makes plain Verlaine's star status on the scene: he is also perceived to be the band's organizing force. When he reaches the point of his arrival in New York, he says he hung around Hell "but then I didn't see him too much; he was running around his [poetry] circle an' I was working at the Strand Bookstore; same place as Patti." The bookstore gave him opportunities to read and take drugs and opened him to the realization that "people are really doing things. It's not just words; it's a real event that's happening, so to speak." To some extent, Verlaine's entire narrative is about the need for

---

10 Gorman (2001: p. 147).

something to happen: "I'm not disappointed that we haven't signed," he said, "but it's about time now. I mean you have to decide if it's going to be a career or a hobby, and if it's going to be a career, you have to sign."[11]

Betrock positioned his publication in territory adjacent to *Punk* and *Rock Scene*. Like *Rock Scene*, Betrock modeled his approach on fan-mags like *16*. If the Robinsons featured photos of David Byrne shopping for groceries, Betrock ran weekly write-in popularity polls. (Television captured the spot of #1 band in the inaugural issue.) An article on "NY Rock Dress Sense" in the magazine's second issue glossed Television's post-Hell look: "Tom Verlaine cheek bones, and Tom Verlaine eyes. Get them at your nearest hobby and toy store. Clothes — nothing more than functional." If Betrock aimed to consolidate the scene's energies by representing local musicians as already having achieved star status, some tension exists with Verlaine's growing desire to keep himself from being pinned with a New York label: "I mean, NY's a great town," Verlaine said. "Coltrane, Dylan, The Blues Project — but now all they think of is glamour. . . . [T]oo many of them seem overly fixated on someone else — you know the Beatles, Lou Reed, or the Dolls."[12]

Verlaine was already swimming against an historiographic tide. In the effort to define the new wave, the *Voice*'s Wolcott again offered the most thoughtful

---

11 Verlaine (1976).
12 Verlaine (1976).

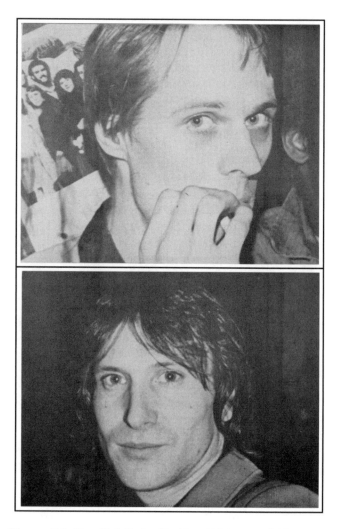

Figure 5.1 *New York Rocker* #3, May 1976, centerfold pin-up. Lloyd, Ficca, Smith. Courtesy Andy Schwartz/*New York Rocker*

Photo by Guillemette Barbet. Clockwise from top left: Verlaine,

criticism at this juncture. Taking a genealogical approach that would become standard over time, he starts with the Velvets, describing Patti Smith, Roxy Music, David Bowie, the Dolls, Talking Heads, and Television all as transatlantic inheritors of their "nihilism of the street." Also at the *Voice*, Christgau took his own stab at pinning down Television and the downtown scene, via a comparison of a night spent watching the Who at Madison Square Garden (his fourteenth time seeing that band) and the next night seeing Television at CBGB's (his eighth time seeing them). While he preferred the intimacy downtown, he still worried that "[Tom] is too sensitive for this crummy Bowery bar," a view that Verlaine would soon endorse. But could Television ever become as big as the Who? "Television is a little too ambitious, and yes, a little too uncommercial, as well," Christgau worried. "I don't think they're capable of a statement as powerful as 'Baba O'Riley' at the Garden last Thursday."[13]

Christgau suggests the degree to which CB's was becoming a critics' bar as much as it belonged to the bands. Its regulars also included a bevy of photographers, filmmakers, and other visual artists. Just as the '60s downtown scene had crossed disciplinary lines, so the new "punk" ethos drew on and borrowed from other arts scenes in adjacent neighborhoods. The first show curated by Jeffrey Deitch in 1975, for instance, which helped launch nearby TriBeCa as an artists' neighborhood, featured Warhol-influenced "artists who made the practice of art inseparable from their

---

13 Christgau (1976).

actual lives — a life performance," the same sentiment
Hell had expressed about the Dolls and tapped when
he conceptualized Television's image. Deitch's show
included work by Marc Miller and others who directly
engaged the CBGB's scene.[14] Commercial rock photographers such as Godlis and Bob Gruen also hung
out at CB's, and Roberta Bayley leveraged photos
of the Ramones and other local bands into a career.
As a result, CB's early period is thoroughly documented, often by prodigious talent. John Rockwell,
who famously attended shows at CBGB's wearing a
suit and bowtie, noted in the summer of '76 that CB's
"has its palpable attractions for writers who might have
grown up in clubs but who now find themselves forced
to cover a never-ending circuit of concerts in indoor
arenas and outdoor stadiums."[15] Hanging out became
a way for critics, artists, and photographers to maintain
a sense of adolescent danger and belonging.

By early 1976, with crowds continuing to grow,
some writers were already expressing nostalgia for
the club's earlier days, when Hilly stocked bookcases
near the entrance and provided a homier feel. The
days of haggling with Roberta Bayley to get in the
door without paying were coming to an end. And
Television, who played monthly four-night stands
between January and May, was already starting to
position its members as the scene's founding fathers,

---

14 For more on Deitch's show and Miller's brilliant photo
   collaboration "Bettie Visits CBGB" see http://98bowery.com/
15 Rockwell (1976c).

now too big for the bar. In Verlaine's inaugural profile in *New York Rocker*, he highlighted his own role in "stumbl[ing] upon CBGBs." Even Richard Hell, no longer in the band, was locating Television's historic position as punk's vanguard; in a piece on the Ramones he wrote for *Hit Parader* in 1976 he noted that the band was one of a half dozen drawn to the Bowery by "Television's 'success' there in late 1974."[16]

Verlaine's sense that his band was "made for a bigger stage" depended on catching the same train out that Patti was on. The pressure was increased, too, by label interest in other CB's bands. In January, Richard Hell recorded demos with the Heartbreakers, including a version of "Blank Generation." Blondie's act was tightening as it debuted a new five-piece format on Valentine's Day. The group had attracted the attention of Marty Thau, the Dolls' first producer, who would eventually help Harry and company land a nationally distributed single and sign them to his own label for a full album that summer. Seymour Stein of Sire Records had put the Ramones under contract the previous November and would shortly get Talking Heads too, based on demos they recorded in April. Richard Hell would leave the Heartbreakers and assemble a new band, the Voidoids, debuting at CBGB's late that year after releasing an EP on Ork Records.

As downtown acts groped around for their own ways to mainstream attention, and with Patti touring the country in the early part of that year, Verlaine and

16 Hell (2001: p. 41).

Lanier, left behind, recorded a new set of Television demos to give to Clive Davis. Two years had passed since the band had played its first gigs at the Townhouse Theater and CBGB's. A year and a half had passed since Richard Williams had heard them play the Truck and Warehouse show, and over a year had gone by since the failed Eno sessions for Island. The band had matured considerably since then, and Lanier knew them better than Eno had. His demos were "warmer," as Verlaine put it later. The songs they recorded were "Torn Curtain," "I Don't Care," "Guiding Light," and "O Mi Amore": two old, two new, two up tempo, and two slow burners, two that would make it onto *Marquee Moon* and two that would be left on the cutting room floor. Davis's Arista showed interest; Sire and Atlantic were also sniffing around, but the former offered too little and the latter thought the band was from another planet. When Davis finally offered them a contract, they passed, worried about direct competition with Patti. By the end of the summer, though, they had finally found a match: Elektra, home of the Doors, Love, the Stooges, and *Nuggets*. Danny Fields helped arrange a private set at CB's for Elektra's Karin Berg, who signed them near the end of July.[17] The deal called for a second album within a year.[18]

If Verlaine was beginning to distance himself from the underground, some there returned his disdain. "The truth was," Lisa Robinson would recall, some

17 Robbins (2001).
18 Gholson (1976).

of "these bands didn't like each other very much."[19] One newcomer, the streetwise rocker Willy DeVille, was infuriated when Terry Ork wouldn't book "just another white blues band." He appealed to Hilly on behalf of his band, Mink DeVille. "It was like a school of vampires," he said of the CB's scene a decade later.[20] Mink DeVille's first gig almost resulted in a rumble with the Ramones, and DeVille, whose music more fully engaged the Latino Lower East Side than most CB's bands, would later disparage the rest of the punk scene to reporters: "Yeah, the Blank Generation — I understand what guys like Tom Verlaine and Richard Hell are talking about," he told a writer from *NME* in 1977, "but they're fuckin' rich kids from private schools in New Jersey. Personally I live close enough to the void that I don't have to flirt with it."[21]

Verlaine also rubbed the critic Lester Bangs the wrong way, resulting in long-standing friction. Bangs, who quit *Creem* and moved to New York in mid-'76, was eager to enter the scene. He loved the Ramones but thought Talking Heads were preppy nerds and that Television sounded like San Francisco psychedelia warmed over. "*This* is punk?" he asked on first seeing them.[22] Though he later warmed to CBGB's, he never gained affection for Verlaine. Being a Television fan seemed to be prerequisite for admission to the scene's inner circle, which

19 Robinson (2002).
20 Kozak (1988: p. 65).
21 Miles (1977).
22 DeRogatis (2000: p. 120).

turned him off, and he thought Television's shows, filled with worshipful fans, were church-like.[23] "[E]verybody had been telling me for three years they're the new Velvet Underground, y'know?" he told fellow critic Richard Meltzer. "And I mean they reminded me so much of the Grateful Dead, just boring solos, y'know, . . . endless, laborious climbing up in the scales, then get to the top and there'd be a moment of silence and everybody in the crowd would go berserk applauding, ha!" Bangs was also miffed by an awkward dinner with Verlaine and Patti Smith. "Who gives a fuck what I think of your fuckin' band, let's just be friends," Bangs demanded, but Verlaine remained reserved. Bangs later heard from Peter Laughner that Verlaine didn't think he'd "make it" in New York, for which Bangs never forgave him. For the most part they'd pass in the street without acknowledging one another. He "always pretends that he doesn't see me, y'know," Bangs told Meltzer, "he's a weird *snob*!"[24] Asked about the stand-off as late as '79, Verlaine said: "I don't know if I'd recognize him. I met him, like, twice about four years ago."[25]

Tension within the original CB's scene escalated in March, when perceived homophobic heckling from the Dictators' singer, Handsome Dick Manitoba, led Wayne County to clobber him with a mic stand, resulting in Manitoba hauled off to the ER with a broken collarbone. Fields reported that Manitoba had been

23 Bangs (1976).
24 Taped conversation, in Meltzer (2000: pp. 337–8).
25 Trakin (1979).

insulting performers for weeks and that some thought he deserved it, but the incident caused rifts among the club's regulars. Benefit shows were held on both sides (three out of four Ramones performed on Wayne's behalf, but Joey abstained).[26] Newcomer Bangs threw himself into the fray, championing Manitoba against what he called the "faggot mafia" that secretly ruled the downtown scene, and which he planned to expose in a *Punk* magazine piece that would also trash Television, though he perhaps wisely had the editors kill the article before it could run.

In May, the Ramones became the second CB's band to release an album. *New York Rocker* ran the glossy national ad campaign. Television, though, remained "the stars of the scene," and Verlaine its "reigning sex symbol," in the *News*'s estimation. ("Don't see them if you're on speed," the reporter added helpfully.[27]) Through the summer of 1976, just as the nation was celebrating its bicentennial birthday, the band performed steadily at CB's. Verlaine and Smith published a small volume of poems together, called *The Night*. The poems' temperature was high — riddled with references to arson and "High gloss lipstick kiss[es]" while sirens and flames blared. But their romantic relationship had finally run its course. That March Patti had met Fred "Sonic" Smith, a member of the proto-punk Detroit legends the MC5, and kicked off an entanglement that would, eventually, lead to

---

26 County (1995: pp. 109–10).
27 Wadsley (1976).

marriage and her relocation to Michigan, where she would withdraw from public view for a decade and a half, until her husband's death in 1994.

With a contract secured in July, the band took off nearly the rest of the year from live performance while they prepared to record. Verlaine worried about marketability and thought the local brand might prove a stumbling block. "I don't think we're an inaccessible New York band," he told one interviewer on the eve of signing with Elektra. "I think we've got a lot of commercial potential, given the right company support."[28] Once the contract was settled, the band selected producer Andy Johns, who was best known as engineer for most of Led Zeppelin's records, to engineer and co-produce their debut. Verlaine said he was drawn to Johns out of admiration of his work on the Stones' 1973 *Goats Heads Soup*. After spending November in the studio, they emerged via a lavish photo spread for the December *New York Rocker* and five year-end shows, culminating in full houses at CBGB's on 30 December (300 people) and a sold-out show to 3,000 the following night at the Palladium, where they shared a bill with Patti Smith and John Cale.[29] Only a decade had passed since Cale was on his way up with the Velvets. Now, on the eve of *Marquee Moon*'s release, Television — so frequently compared to Cale's former band — were *New York Rocker*'s Band of the Year, poised at last to break out of the downtown unerground.

---

28 Strick (1976).
29 Rockwell (1976b).

6
Marquee Moon

Electricity kills the subtle mysteries of the city night —
and then resurrects them in new forms.
> — *William Chapman Sharpe*,
> New York Nocturne *(2008)*

I like thinking of myself as invisible.
> — *Tom Verlaine*, Spin, *1987*

In November 1976, Television and Andy Johns spent
three weeks recording *Marquee Moon* at A&R Studios
on 48th Street. Opened by Phil Ramone in 1960, the
studio still had its original soundboard. Ramone had
since expanded operations, taking over a Columbia
Records studio on Seventh Avenue, where he'd
recently engineered Dylan's *Blood on the Tracks*. But
he continued to lease the 48th Street space for a price
the band could afford on its budget from Elektra. The
studio may have been run down — "How can I work in
a place like this?" Johns repeatedly asked — but it was
storied: Coltrane had recorded there, as had Dylan,
Van Morrison, and the Velvet Underground.

Johns had no prior knowledge of the band and had never heard them perform before entering the studio. Verlaine had been attracted to him because he remained relatively invisible as a producer, "getting really decent overall rock sounds without messing with the arrangements," Verlaine told a writer for *Crawdaddy!*. The band wanted to keep arrangements minimal, even more stripped down than the Stones had on *Goats Head Soup*: "no horns, no strings, no synthesizers, no acoustic guitar."[1] The result would approximate their live sound, foregrounding the friction between Lloyd's and Verlaine's guitars. Verlaine later ascribed the sessions' success to Johns being so "performance oriented — he recognized the hot take."[2] The band had spent the better part of fall '76 in rehearsal, sharpening the songs: "We had to learn to play all of our songs without the vocals because that's the way you make a record," Lloyd told *New York Rocker*. "Where I would normally play a certain basic riff and then throw frills around it, we had to condition ourselves to know the basics first." The result was a tighter sound on all the songs. "It's not that there is less experimentation going on, it's just that everything is clear in our heads as to the way we want it to sound."[3]

Settling in with Johns required acclimation on all sides. "My first impression was that they couldn't play and couldn't sing and the music was very bizarre,"

---

1 Elliot (1977).
2 Demorest (1977).
3 Gholson (1976).

Johns said later. He also had to bring in equipment to supplement the outdated studio's set-up. Lloyd recalled that Johns had set up the drums without input from the band and when he played back the initial recordings, "by God, out of the speakers, out of Billy Ficca's drums, came John Bonham's drum sound! Tom looked at me, and looked at Fred and Billy. Billy was like, 'It sounds pretty good to me,' and Tom's like, 'No, no, no, no, no. You've got to undo all of this.'" When Verlaine described the sound he wanted, Johns responded: "Oh, this must be like a Velvets thing, right? It's New York thing, right?'"[4] Verlaine wanted to keep studio gimmickry minimal, sticking with a live sound: "clean Fender guitars." Lloyd pushed the envelope a little more, double-tracking his parts, repeating his lead and rhythm lines virtually note for note: "When Andy Johns began recording us I suggested that I could double my parts," Lloyd recalled, an idea he took from Phil Spector and the Beatles. On some songs he layered his parts even further — up to eight tracks on "Guiding Light."[5] What resulted is the shimmering, chorused quality of the album's guitar sounds. Verlaine approved of the results, agreeing that the doubling "sounds better than just a little delay, left and right," he later told *Guitar World* magazine.[6] Other effects were subtle: Johns swung a mic like a lasso while Lloyd

4 Robbins (2001).
5 Lloyd, "Ask Richard."
6 Mengaziol (1981).

played his part for "Elevation."[7] Otherwise the takes were relatively straightforward. After the first week recording, Johns jaunted to California, returning to mix after the band had done a good portion of the production legwork. When he heard what they'd done, according to Verlaine, he said, "Jesus, this is great!"[8]

For the album's cover the group went to Mapplethorpe, who had shot the cover of *Horses*. The photograph they ultimately selected situates Verlaine a step in front of the rest of the band, with Lloyd staggered next, then Smith, and Ficca receding farthest into the background. Everyone looks rather serious, muscles tensed, veins bulging on the back of hands. Only Ficca approaches anything like a smile. Verlaine's right hand crosses his body; his left is held up in front of him as if he's about to offer something to the viewer, but his hand is empty, his fist slightly clenched. He could just as easily be withholding something from you as offering.

When Mapplethorpe gave the band the contact prints, Lloyd took the band's favorite shot to a Times Square print shop and asked for color Xeroxes — still a rarity in 1976 — so the band members could each take a copy home to mull over. The first few came out oddly colored, but Lloyd asked to keep them and told the worker to make several more copies "while turning the knobs with his eyes closed." It was like a Warhol thing, he thought to himself, recalling Terry

---

7 Lloyd, "Ask Richard."
8 Licht (2003).

Ork's work on Warhol's screenprint multiples. When he took the distorted images back to the band, they chose one of the altered versions over Mapplethorpe's original, which Fred Smith framed and kept in his possession.[9] The final result looks like reception on a color television with the contrast slightly off. Or perhaps you could call it a double exposure.

Marquee Moon is a nocturnal album, set largely out of doors. But in the era before the Walkman, these are experiences and scenes to be imagined from the comfort of an interior space with a stereo system. While it's absolutely possible in 2011 to listen to this album while actually walking the streets of lower Manhattan after midnight — an experience I'd recommend — that possibility didn't exist for most in 1977, though Nick Kent would later describe listening to an advance tape of the album on a portable recorder as he stumbled through London's smack houses.[10] For most of the original release's listeners, the album began by fitting the disc on your turntable's spindle, setting the grooves spinning, and lowering the needle. Then, when the grind of "See No Evil" kicked in, you'd *imagine* yourself walking through a semi-medieval downtown landscape, by turns bright and doubly dark.

Maybe you'd follow along with the lyrics, printed on the sleeve. Making sense of Verlaine's lyrics has always been a bit of a dangerous proposition: their obscurity is a good part of Television's mystique, and

---

9 Lloyd (2007), email to Casey.
10 Kent (2010: p 314).

the act of deciphering — and arguing with friends about — their meanings remains one of the album's many pleasures. If you knew these songs live before you heard them on vinyl, or if you never bothered to read the lyrics, you might already have formed phrases of your own to fill in where you couldn't make out what Verlaine was saying. "I couldn't understand a single word [of] Verlaine's strangled vocals," Peter Laughner said of seeing Television live before they'd recorded, "but the feelings came on like razors and methadrine. His singing voice has this marvelous quality of slurring all dictions into what becomes distortions of actual lines, so that without a lyric sheet you can come away with a whole other song . . . which means you're doing a third of the work."[11] Adding to this sense, Verlaine's lyrics, as Hell's had been, were fueled by puns and double-entendres, filled with riddles and word games, inside jokes: "Get it?" he asks before launching into the final section of "See No Evil," as if he's calling on you to make sense of things or join him in a joke. Asked by *Punk* magazine about the lyrics, Verlaine called them atmospheric: "I mean, you don't have to say what you mean to get across." Lloyd chimed in: "It's like you say five words and you mean the sixth." Verlaine: "Right."[12] In such moments, Verlaine's project is compatible with a post-Cagean conceptualism that would bring audiences to some awareness of ways they participate in meaning-making, though in rock

---

11 Laughner (1977).
12 *"Punk* Talks."

'n' roll that process is less overt than in other forms of performance Cage inspired.

Verlaine's long engagement with poetry, especially in this period, would seem to authorize *some* literary critical self-indulgence. His lyrics, after all, are a main reason Television's contemporaries referred to the band as cerebral or intellectual, though they were sometimes also dismissed as inscrutable LSD after-effects whose meaning was only plain to their author. The lyrics sheet itself creates some tension on this front: it offers an invitation to interpretation, not simply by printing the words, but because it sometimes obscures more than it illuminates. One thing's printed, but Tom seems to sing another. At times it seems like we're being misdirected by homophonic phrases (the way Kurt Cobain would later print "find my nest of salt" for what sounded more like "feminist assault" on Nirvana's "All Apologies"). In terms of poetic schools, Verlaine's lyrical style, despite some comparability to the New York School, relates more closely to the French poets he and Hell — and other contemporaries — had been steeped in: *Marquee Moon*'s urban nocturne derives from long traditions of bohemian decadence, not so far removed from Ginsberg's celebrations of "Negro streets at dawn" and other presumed danger zones. *Marquee Moon* isn't a concept album, but it has a consistent geography overtly identified with lower Manhattan, and as such lends itself to a coherent reading as a song cycle.

Television's New York settings are, as Patti Smith suggested in her earliest criticism on the band, relentlessly adolescent. They occupy the parts of town most resistant to the bright lights that had long since conquered New York's night; his characters seem consciously to flee overlit areas for deeper shadows. The area below 14th Street seemed like the special province of the young and wild at night, a sense exacerbated by the city's financial crisis, which left much of downtown empty and dark. "I remember standing at windows," remembered Roberta Bayley, "looking out over the Lower East Side, and feeling that the whole city was infested, and crumbling, but wonderful."[13] In such an environment, friends roamed in packs, searching for adventure, for trouble, but also for a sense of self, or perhaps even for the purity of egoless transcendence over the urban surround. If *Marquee Moon* celebrates relentless adolescence in the mode of the urban pastoral, it also looks for visionary truth through Rimbaud's prescription of sensory derangement. Such wandering and transcendental flashes are as propulsive as *Marquee Moon*'s opening riff.

Side A

"See No Evil"

It's one of the great starts to a rock 'n' roll album ever. For the first five seconds we're at the starting line, engine revving, three times from the left. In the fourth measure the bass line enters on the right, an

---

13 Savage (2010: p. 138).

octave higher than we'd expect, as if to say "Ready, Set, Go!" Like most Television songs this one starts with an extended introduction, a sense of anticipation, hesitation, building tension. Then, we're off, though the stress falling on the first and third beats creates a slightly syncopated sense of lurching. The music is repetitive, churning, the sounds of machinery, the lead guitar rolling on the right hand side like a power saw cutting pavement. It's the same grinding force Eno poured into the opening track of his solo debut, "Needle in the Camel's Eye." Ficca's drumming leaves behind blues structures generally and specifically departs from early versions of the song that were still tied to Byrds-like go-go beats. Then, an opening lyric, in Verlaine's strained, nasal harangue, that runs counter to the sense of waiting we've already experienced: "What I want / I want NOW."

Like live staples that *didn't* make it onto the album — "O Mi Amore" and especially their cover of the Elevators' "Fire Engine" — "See No Evil" suggests an urban landscape in the clack of a subway or the Doppler Effect of a passing ambulance or firetruck. It recalls the New York Dolls, but only the slightest hint of a campy lisp remains in the backing chorus. Rather, as they have throughout the album, the band has worked to strip away what Verlaine called "reference points," gestures or figures that reassure listeners by recalling the familiar sounds of an earlier era. The song does bear some similarity to the sound of '66, and you might even think it's a Yardbirds cover. (Their "Train Kept A-Rollin'" anticipated Ficca's opening drum line on "Fire Engine.") But Television strips away the Yardbirds' rootsiness to produce this New York noir: no harmonicas here. The territory we're in is nervous, angular, to use adjectives contemporaries often applied to them. The sound's industrial, even: the Ficca/Smith rhythm section is "a fist punching metal rivets of sound," as Nick Kent wrote. The buzzsaw of Verlaine's "soaring [vocal] screech at the fadeout" suggests the united howling of "what sounds like about 25 over-dubbed Verlaines screaming."[14] We're not being warned that the train is coming, as in old blues songs. We're in the front car, watching the tracks disappear beneath us as we go.

With "See No Evil," *Marquee Moon* begins not quite out of doors, but with a desire to exit, a fantasy of escaping to the hills. That desire is complex: "What I want / I want NOW / and it's a whole lot more / than 'anyhow.'" Lines are being drawn in the sand. The scare quotes on 'anyhow' are the first instance on the lyrics sheet of a pattern that recurs — a distancing effect, making a portion of the lyrics suspect even to their speaker. "Anyhow" seems to be a synonym here for "good enough," and recalls comments Verlaine made to *Creem* on the album's release: "I do think in terms of good and evil," he said. "Evil is an attitude that comes over a person who refuses to discriminate. There was a California expression: 'It's all the same.' Drinking a glass of water or cutting a leg off, 'Oh, it's all the same.'"[15]

---

14 Wolcott (1977); Laughner (1977).
15 Demorest (1977).

Wanting a lot isn't the same as being indiscriminate; it's a sentiment diametrically opposed to the resignation in "I Don't Care," the early Television favorite that would resurface on *Adventure* as "Careful." In that song Verlaine sings "I don't care" over and over, a statement of apolitical detachment from the American 1970s, a decade of perpetual crisis: Watergate, Vietnam, New York's fiscal quicksand. In "See No Evil," Verlaine's speaker doesn't retreat, defeated. "No don't say doom," he warns. Rather, he's all action, wanting to "fly / fly a fountain" or "jumpjumpjump / jump a mountain," even as the stutter suggests stasis. Perhaps the sense of action remains fantasy after all.

The second verse, Ficca pulling us along like a conveyer belt, offers the song's best wordplay, a few lines among Verlaine's wittiest: "I get ideas / I get a notion," he sings, another hint of his indebtedness to conceptualism: "I want a nice little boat / made out of ocean." The "notion" here seems to be paradox: can you stay afloat in a vessel made out of the stuff it's meant to keep out? This "nice little boat," impossible and imaginary, is the song's — and the album's — first reference to sea-going, and seems significant in that regard. These images will accumulate, especially on the album's second side, when the action seems to be set on the waterfront: in "Elevation," the Side B opener, we'll find the singer sleeping "light / on these shores tonight"; from "Guiding Light": "Darling Darling / Do we part like the seas"; from "Prove It": "The docks / the clocks," "the cave / the waves." And the list goes on. Verlaine's paradoxical "nice little boat / made out of ocean" relates to all of these in suggestive ways. The desire for something impossible persists through all the other sea images. What are you waiting for, sleeping there on the shore, or strolling the waterfront with an eye on the clock? "What I want / I want NOW" may be an aggressive way to start an album, but that desire is countered at every turn by a competing sense of anticipation, longing, unfilled possibility.

That sense of hesitation will be borne out over the entire album as the singer seems caught in a tug-of-war with something or someone. Perhaps the speaker argues with himself: "I get your point. / You're so sharp," the song's sharpest pun, is followed up immediately by Verlaine's most inscrutable lyric: "Getting good reactions / with your 'BeBo' talk." What "BeBo" is meant to signify remains a mystery. Is it "Be Bop," meaning his interlocutor is jive talking, talking smack? Is it a homophone for Patti Smith's favorite self-referential play on words: "Babel/babble"? Is he actually saying "when your people talk," despite what's printed on the lyrics sheet? The move from a finely honed lyric in the point/sharp pun to something this inscrutable might be offputting, if he weren't couching it in a line that attacks someone for empty speech that wins acclaim.

At precisely this point the lyrics give way to Lloyd's first solo, supplanting the vocals just when words fail. Prefiguring most of the solos to follow on the album, Lloyd runs up, up, up — following a major scale but falling back slightly after each step. Adding to the sense of climbing, anticipation, waiting, desire, this pattern will have its fullest effect on the album's title track, with a slight alteration as Verlaine's mixolydian mode — lowering the seventh by half a step — prolongs the wait to the last possible moment. In "See No Evil," however, Lloyd brings the solo through a full octave of gradual climbing, starts and stops, before unleashing a blues-inflected riff, Berry-via-Beck, that, compared with the minimalist repetition and restraint elsewhere in the song feels like he's cleaning out his arsenal.

"See No Evil" has been read as a rejoinder to Hell's supposed nihilism in "Blank Generation," primarily on the grounds of Verlaine's disavowal of "destructive urges."[16] But the two songs share more than separates them. In spite of Lester Bangs's famous reproach to Hell for what seemed a constant death wish, or Wolcott's reading of "Blank Generation" as a smack-induced "nod-off anthem," Hell's insistence that the "blank" in "blank generation" stands for possibility aligns him with Verlaine's sentiments here. Verlaine closes "See No Evil" by replacing the opening's fantasies of flight with a limitless terrain, "runnin wild with the one I love." The renegade sensation is contagious, an imperative to go and do likewise. "Pull down the future with the one you love," he repeats as the song ends. It's creative and destructive all at once. Is he still talking to the same antagonist or interlocutor? Or has he moved from an intimate conversation to a more inclusive stance, letting us in as listeners?

---

16 Mitchell (2006: p. 64).

"Venus"

If the opening track suggested urban out-of-doors, on "Venus" the landscape is explicitly defined as New York's.

One of the oldest songs in Television's repertoire, "Venus" existed in an acoustic version dating all the way back to Verlaine's ventures into Greenwich Village folk clubs, pre-Neon Boys, pre-Reno Sweeney. "[H]ardcore Televisionaries will be pleased that 'Venus de Milo' is on the album," Wolcott wrote in his review for *Hit Parader*, which he composed after just two pre-release listens when Verlaine and Smith brought master tapes to Lisa and Richard Robinson's apartment. "[I]t's to Television what 'The Lady Is A Tramp' is to Sinatra — a signature song. Like 'Tramp' it wears well: I've heard 'Venus de Milo' at least 70 times and have yet to tire of it."[17] John Rockwell, using the album's release as an occasion for a retrospective on the underground's last several years, suggested that Venus "epitomize[d] the whole scene": "the distant, hypersensitive, painfully acute sensibility that permeates the late-night, fluorescent-lit New York landscape."[18] The song starts with nine and a half bars of intro — a full twenty seconds — before Verlaine comes in: more hesitation and anticipation. Ficca establishes a lighter tone than the earliest recorded versions of the song convey: 1-2-cha-cha-cha, whereas the beat in the Island demo had been almost martial.

17 Wolcott (1977).
18 Rockwell (1977a).

The opening lines move us into story-land: "It was a tight toy night." Again we're confronted with a rather obscure phrase. Is it the night or the singer that's tightly wound (in the Warholian sense of being "up-tight")? Or is it just the sort of night that leaves you tightly wound, played with? The phrase is evocative but remains opaque: the alliteration ("tight toy") and the internal rhyme ("tight/night") call attention to the lyrics' status as just words, hinting at Verlaine's obsession with verbal play as much as anything else. But the opening structure lends to storytelling, stage-setting: here the streets are bright, the nocturnal atmosphere established by contrast, as if you need to escape the more brightly lit parts of town and find some darker quarter downtown in which to take solace.

"Broadway looks so medieval": Tim Mitchell suggests Grace Church at Broadway between 10th and 11th Streets as the setting invoked in this line, the clearest signal that the album's world is our own. But I've never biked down Broadway at night, the Woolworth Building's lighted gothic spire looming at the bottommost tip of Manhattan, without thinking of this lyric. The song's geography has a downward sweep that corresponds with the repeated idea of fall/falling: in the third verse the friends wander down Broadway, which after dark, especially amid the nineteenth-century factories and warehouses of SoHo's Cast-iron District, seemed positively abandoned. In the distance, towers hulked: the new World Trade Center looming. The Woolworth, once the epitome of modernity, seems dwarfed, hunchbacked and ancient.

As Lisa Robinson suggests in her memoir of these "Rebel Nights," to downtown's youthful inhabitants in the 1970s, that nighttime world was their own. Whatever SoHo factories remained operational were closed for the night or converted to performance spaces, blocks of seemingly abandoned buildings, inhabited here and there by rogue theater companies, jazz ensembles, early no-wave noisemakers, or underground discos. Street traffic dwindled. A couple old bars catered to loft-livers and nocturnal freaks. The whole lower portions of the city, from the Village to TriBeCa, became a world occupied by the young and the hip, on one hand, or the hopelessly derelict on the other. The line between the two was thin at times.

Of all Television's songs, "Venus" is the one that most overtly participates in one of the dominant trends of New York School poetry: the practice of dropping names of friends and fellow poets into your work to create a sense of community and/or cliquishness. (Contrast Television's oeuvre on this score with Patti Smith's, which brims with names and musical references that invoke a pantheon of Romantic and rock 'n' roll heroes.) The relevant lines from "Venus" offer the album's most poignant reminder, left behind like a scar, of the falling out between Verlaine and Hell. *Falling out*: the word "fell" recurs at the end of the first and third verses, returning in each repetition of the chorus. At the end of the second verse we find "And I felt" where we're previously heard "fell." What is the relationship between falling and feeling? The song's call-and-response structure perpetuates this conflation:

"And I fell."

"DIDJA FEEL LOW?"

To fall is to feel? *Nah. Not at all.* The word "felt" follows the most personal verse, the one with a shout-out, most listeners have assumed, to Richard Hell by name. Though this song predates Television, which means it also predates the end of Hell and Verlaine's friendship, by 1977 the words would have taken on additional meaning for many. If the anecdote about Richard suggesting that the friends dress up like cops is autobiographical — and there's no reason to insist it has to be — the action probably took place during the period of time, in their early twenties, that Verlaine has described as a consistent period of drug use: "From 21 to 23," he later said, "I was using all kinds of hallucinogenics."[19] The specificity of the time frame suggests that he put an end to drug use around the time Television formed, though most of his comments on the subject come retrospectively, after Hell's departure from the band (amid gossip about his heroin use), and perhaps should be taken with a grain of salt. "People who mess with drugs, I can't stand to be around them too long," Verlaine would add in a typical aside, obviously flung in Hell's direction. "Do you still experiment with drugs a lot?" one interviewer asked in 1976. Tom:

> No, not much at all. I wouldn't say really at all. Drugs
> are like . . . if you're intuitive about things or something
> and you take drugs, they make you believe in your own

---

19 Heylin (1993: p. 96).

intuitions more 'cause there's something very nebulous about drugs, and there's something unspeakably true about what you go through with any given drug.[20]

Richard Hell's cameo in "Venus" had its parallels in Verlaine's poetry. In the manuscript for the collection *28TH Century*, which Hell declined to publish following his departure from Television, one poem specifically invokes Hell. In it, Verlaine phones up Hell and tells him the time has come for a planned takeover, of what isn't made clear. Richard responds by taking him less than seriously, and Tom pretends not to be himself.[21] As in this poem, and as in "See No Evil" as well, "Venus" consists of a speaker engaged in dialogue with another character, or in this case a series of them. In the first verse it's "another person who was a little surprised." The second verse begins with a generic second person address: "You know it's all like some new kind of drug." The third verse brings us to a past-tense narration of the episode with Richie/Richard, who suggests they dress up like cops. Two other voices enter the song, though: the band's responses to Verlaine's calls ("I fell." "DIJA FEEL LOW?") and the voice of conscience at the end of the third verse: "But something, something said 'You better not.'" That final bit of dialogue — an internal one between the speaker and a Donald Duck angel sitting on his shoulder — puns on the form of the song itself. When Verlaine sings

---

20 Kugel (1977).
21 Hell Papers, Box 9, Folder 594.

"Something, something . . ." it sounds, even if you've heard the song hundreds of times, as if he's forgotten the lyrics. A moment of disenchantment, it reminds us we're not in lower Manhattan at all; rather, we're caught up in a fantasy about would-be rockstars, a band of friends.

The notion that we're dwelling in the realm of imagination is underscored by the song's central refrain — "I fell into the arms of Venus de Milo" — which works in much the same way as the earlier "boat made out of ocean," given that the Venus de Milo, at least as we know the statue, has no arms at all. "Do those amputated arms beckon? Or repulse?" asked *Creem*'s reviewer, Stephen Demorest. "Do they modestly try to cover her privates? The high ones or the low? Verlaine says: 'The arms of Venus de Milo are everywhere. It's a term for a state of feeling. They're loving arms.'"

What we've fallen into, then, is love. Or emptiness. Or imagination. Which could mean nothing, or everything.

"Friction"

So far Side A's tone has been up, almost optimistic. If this is urban noir, it's also a fun house. Enter "Friction," as the title would suggest, to provide counterpoint and conflict.

The first guitar plays octaves, the drums roll, the second guitar enters with light alarm-bell harmonics followed by cascading downward scales, like skipping rocks over a minor-key waterfall in a Chinese garden, before we get the lyrical throwdown: "I knew it must have been some big setup."

It's tempting to read the placement of this confrontational snarl, hot on the heels of the album's only overt personal reference (generally taken to be a nod to Hell, at that), as personal in some way. "If I ever catch that ventriloquist / I'll squeeze his head right into my fist," Verlaine will sing in a few lines, and you want to know who's the target of this anger. On the Island demo, Hell plays a rough, bouncing bass, and the opening lyric is slightly different: "I knew it must have been some *sweet* set up," suggesting fulfillment and abundance rather than the disillusionment of a "big setup" exposed. In its early versions "Friction" was more of a rocker than it is on the album, its solos unconstrained, Lloyd noodling all over the song's surface. The album version's more controlled, even if the tempo's sped up a bit. Verlaine's sneer on "set up" retains the bite of Wayne County or the Dolls.

Nick Kent, writing in *NME*, saw "Friction" as filling Television fans' expectations for the album, but thought it a little predictable:

> "Friction" is probably the most readily accessible track from this album simply because, with its fairly anarchic, quasi-Velvets feel plus (all important) Verlaine's most pungent methedrine guitar fret-board slaughter, here it'll represent the kind of thing all those weaned on the hype and legend without hearing one note from Television will be expecting . . . "Friction" is just that

— throwaway lyrics — "diction/Friction" etc. — those kind of throwaway rhymes, vicious instrumentation and a perfect climax which has Verlaine vengefully spelling out the title "F-R-I-C-T-I-O-N" slashing his guitar for punctuation.[22]

Actually, the lyrics don't seem throwaway at all. Like the music's evocation of train crossings and warning bells, the lyrics tell us we're in dangerous territory. Once again the danger comes from adolescence itself: "All us boys are going to wind up in jail." Recalling Peter Pan's "I Won't Grow Up," the singer asserts a desire to stave off adulthood: "There's too much contradiction." Nevertheless this is a song about transformations: "How did the snake get out of its skin?" Verlaine's double entendres underwrite the sense of adolescent danger, a key feature of Neon Boys and early Television songs that never saw studio release ("Hot Dog," "Hard On Love," "Love Comes in Spurts," "Horizontal Ascension"). "I just start to spin the tale," Verlaine sings, when "you complain of my DICK [pause] shun." Words ("diction") are no substitute for nagging sexual desires unevenly fulfilled. When Verlaine asks "How does a snake get out of its skin?" he has his own answer: "Here's a depiction," he sings, then leaves words behind as he rips into a chainsaw ascension. To get here we've been through stages of desire: "Gimme friction," the singer pleads. "I dig friction," he promises. "I betcha it's friction,"

_____

22 Kent (1977a).

he anticipates. And only then the "depiction" arrives: aural, not verbal or visual. This moment resembles one from a favorite choice for Television to cover, "Psychotic Reaction," which launches into a solo following the declaration: "And it feels like *this*." Like other references in "Friction" to physical sensation ("My eyes are like telescopes," for instance), the urgency of the skin-shedding "depiction" suggests that friction is physical as much as metaphorical, the kind of friction that takes place in a car parked off the main road, the dry humping that substitutes for teenage foreplay.

Nagging sexual desires unevenly fulfilled. What could be more adolescent? What better characterization of the energy that drives you into city streets at night?

"Marquee Moon"

The title track brings the sublime moment all Side A has worked toward. Routinely praised since its release as one of the great guitar songs of all time, it simmers and then boils for close to ten minutes. The original LP version fades at 9:58, necessary to preserve the album's sound quality; like "Little Johnny Jewel" the track would also be spread over both sides of a 7-inch single. On remastered CD and vinyl reissues the song is closer to eleven minutes. "Conceived at a time when rock tracks lasting over ten minutes are somewhere sunk deep below the subterranean depths of contempt,"

Kent wrote, "'Marquee Moon' is as riveting a piece of music as I've heard since the halcyon days of . . . oh, God knows too many years have elapsed."[23]

Opening with an off-beat interplay between the two guitars, "like voices [conversing] across the railroad tracks,"[24] the sixteen-bar intro allows each instrument to enter individually, creating the effect of a chamber piece, or the beginning of an old musical in which the combined sounds of street noise eventually form a symphonic overture. Alarm systems overlay a bass line thumping from a passing car. Sirens blend as fire trucks head in opposite directions. Partially set in a darkened cemetery that could be rural as easily as it could sit on lower Broadway, the song also invokes the Great White Way, your name in Times Square's lights. "Moonlight drips on 42nd Street," Verlaine mumbles at the start of a live version from early '75, recorded at CBGB's. But the title could also refer to London's famous Marquee club, to the Stones and Yardbirds what CB's was to Television. As on the rest of the album, the setting is shadowy, the double darkness offset by moonlight and lightning. "Marquee Moon" helps to clarify that the antagonistic pairs running through all side A's songs are figures of doubling. Is there a coherent self behind these songs? Can we exist without reflection? If the other songs to this point have all featured traveling companions, on this one the singer journeys solo.

"Marquee Moon" is structured on a backward

---

23 Kent (1977a).
24 Wolcott (1977).

glance: "I remember," it opens as the rhythm section carries us forward on a mechanical current. The voice is a survivor's, someone who remains to tell the tale, like Job or Melville's Ishmael. Combined with the gothic setting, the glance back prepares us for the dev-il-at-the-crossroads story to follow. Robert Johnson's "Crossroads Blues" is a key precursor, revived by Cream in 1968 and made one of rock's great singles. "Marquee Moon" could almost be a blues lyric or a folk ballad, but it abandons the formal repetition of either form for a straightforward, linear progression, a story building verse by verse, which will eventually climax in something much freakier than a blues solo.

As the song moves forward, the speaker, who's been waiting/hesitating, finally makes a break — "I ain't waiting" — only to be met by "a man / down at the tracks." The speaker asks for advice: "How do you not go mad?" And the man replies: "Look here, junior, don't you be so happy / And for Heaven's sake don't you be so sad." The use of opposite extremes here, both of which are off limits, echoes the pairing a few lines earlier: "the kiss of death, the embrace of life." How to hold on to both sides, to avoid being absorbed by one or the other?

Ken Emerson, reviewing the album for the *Voice*, reads it primarily through this preoccupation with doubling (the darkness doubles, and words like *listening* and *hearing* are paired). For Emerson, this recurring feature is a balancing act, which he sees as evidence that Television has already grown up, perhaps in spite of themselves.[25] (It could also derive from Verlaine's experience as an fraternal twin.) Yet the balance Emerson sees is itself offset by something extrasensory and unsettling: "I was listening / listening to the rain / I was hearing / hearing something else." If "listening" and "hearing" are doubles, as Emerson suggests, the contrast *between* listening and hearing emphasizes distinction. What is it we're waiting for, straining to tune in?

As warning bells gather force, the man at the crossroads is joined, in the next verse, by what Kent called "various twilight loony rejects from *King Lear*" who pull up in a Cadillac and motion for the speaker to climb in. They'll ferry him, in this pimped-out Styx-crossing transport, to the cemetery from whence they've come. When the singer obliges, apparently embracing death, the Cadillac putters back to the graveyard, but our hero has the final laugh, getting "out again" before it's too late. Whatever deal with the devil may have gone down, the narrator's going to live to see another day, having cheated the Reaper.

The song's hardly over, though. We've been through all the verses in the song's first four minutes; one more chorus, and then: back to the start? The singer still insists he's not waiting, but now waiting is exactly what we have to do. At 4:50 we get the stirrings of Tom's solo, which unfolds at roughly half Lloyd's speed. His line rings, tentatively, in multiple directions, like a junebug beating against the glass, until at just past the seven-minute mark he finds some release by climbing

---

25 Emerson (1977).

scales, doubled the second time around by Lloyd's harmonies a third higher. This signature scale-climb was drawn from an older Television song, "Change Your Channels," a driving highlight of the band's early sets. Back then it was used to bring things to a fever pitch. Here the progression also pushes toward climax, but backs off repeatedly. Once. Twice. The third time up, the axes chop in unison: *do*-2-3-rest, *do*-2-3-rest, *re*-2-3-rest, *re*-2-3-rest, *mi*-2-3-rest, *mi*-2-3-rest, and so on, two measures per step, leading up this fourteen-measure hillside like Fraulein Maria's evil twin. As it builds, the drums hit double time, the bass glides an upward slide, and if you listen closely you'll catch a dissonant current multi-tracked beneath it all. Then, just as the scale finally approaches completion, what seemed at first to be a straight-forward major scale has its mixolydian moment, the half-step "gotcha" at the end, one final deferral before a burst of harmonics scatter like a shower of "little bells,"[26] "droplets of electricity,"[27] bluebirds singing.

Nick Kent tied the scattered guitar lines that follow the climax to Richard Thompson's playing on Fairport Convention's eleven-minute epic rendition of the traditional folk song "A Sailor's Life," from the 1969 classic *Unhalfbricking*. The cymbals' rolling thunder adds to the echo. It's an unlikley comparison, but Verlaine does bear some similarity to Thompson, as he does to Neil Young and Jerry Garcia. Fairport's folk song

---

26 Demorest (1978).
27 Kent (1977a).

works well as an earnest counterpoint to Television's nervous energy. The comparison also helps us hear how "Marquee Moon" overwrites as urban pastoral both the crossroads song *and* the seafaring tale, the latter being another of the album's consistent motifs. To be adrift in the nocturnal cityscape of "Marquee Moon" is very much like being at sea; the characters on *Marquee Moon*, if you take in the album's action as a whole, move gradually toward the waterfront, pulled by a sort of Melvillean magnetism. As the soaring climax finishes, "Marquee Moon" returns to the familiar ground of the song's opening verse. The record still spins. Regarding the fade that originally closed the LP's first side, Lloyd told *New York Rocker*: "I think it's mood-evoking in a way that the voice starts to come in and then just fades away. It gives you the conception that the song never really ends."[28] On the reissues, the restored version of the track fades at 10:40 over the whisper of rolling piano arpeggios, a Cadillac idling, waves moving back out to sea.

Side B

"Elevation"

On one hand, anything to follow "Marquee Moon," once you turn over the platter and start Side B, will be a coming down: How to match the dizzying climb of Lloyd's and Verlaine's intertwined solos on the title

---

28 "Television" (1977).

track? Though Side B is in general a little mellower than the first four songs, rather than a letdown we're offered a self-referential meditation on "Elevation." Are your senses sufficiently deranged following the heights of Side A?

We may get a meditation on Television as well. It's impossible to know who started the rumor that Verlaine actually substitutes the word "Television" for the word "Elevation" in the refrain: "Elevation don't go to my head." But someone jumped on that possibility as soon as the record was released, if not before. Kent was just one of the critics to pounce: "The song again is beautiful, proudly contagious with a chorus that lodges itself in your subconscious like a bullet in the skull — 'Elevation don't go to my head' repeated thrice until on the third line a latent ghost-like voice transmutes 'Elevation' into 'Television.'"[29] Maybe the band promoted the rumor themselves. In the months after the record was released, their answer was a uniform denial. As Lloyd told *New York Rocker*: "There's a mechanical harmonizer that adds the third, fifth and octave of a voice. Just on the word 'elevation' to fill it out." When asked if Tom sings "Television, don't go to my head," Lloyd answered: "No, he really doesn't say that. We even thought so when it was happening and he articulated it as best he could. It's just magic or something."[30] Later writers would assume the studio tweaking was meant

---

29 Kent (1997a).
30 "Television" (1977).

to emphasize the conflation of band name and song title,[31] and certainly those who wanted to could hear him acknowledge the band's impact on his personality ("Television, don't go to my head"). "The last word / is the lost word," the song begins, almost as if to offer a challenge: Which word is lost? The song title or the band name?

Given the heights of "Marquee Moon," it's hardly surprising to find ourselves dizzy as side two starts. The guitars open like alarm bells and Fred Smith takes the melody on bass, inverting typical roles and emphasizing disorientation. And yet the song isn't set on a mountaintop at all, but on "these shores." The speaker "sleep[s] light" and "live[s] light," the repetition of "light" suggesting light-headedness, but also speaking to the images of light and dark that fill side one and preparing us for the "Guiding Light" of the next track. Sleeping light and living light aren't exactly the same thing: one suggests insomnia and mental burdens, the other a feeling that you could care less. At some point in the song, the address changes from first person singular to second person: "Now you give me no trouble / You give me no help," Verlaine sings, suggesting perfect balance in his addressee's indifference. As Tim Mitchell points out, "Elevation," one of the newest songs on the record, was written in the midst of Verlaine's breakup with Patti Smith. In a live version caught on tape the

---

31 Robbins (2001). Lloyd, though not quoted outright, is the implied source.

previous spring, he includes a lyric that would be dropped by the time they recorded the album: "I tell you, darling, how you must make me fade / I wish I'd never, never been wed."[32] The song retains a haunted quality, once again bracketed by Verlaine's high guitar chops that sound like warning signals. Lloyd's solo is positively plaintive.

Mitchell also notes the similarity between Verlaine's lyric and Baudelaire's poem "Élévation," from the infamous collection *Flowers of Evil* (1857). That poem also invokes bodies of water and upward motion: the speaker's soul rises above lakes and vales, passing clouds as it rises above this mortal sphere and leaves the earth's miasma and all concerns behind. Purification will be found in ethereal realms. Baudelaire's poem is a fantasy of losing one's ego, a fitting counterpart to Verlaine's play on "don't go to my head." But the pun preserves a sense of literal dizziness and disorientation, and in doing so keeps Verlaine's speaker from absolute transcendence. Instead of floating away into the atmosphere, he haunts the shoreline like a hermit in search of a hut. The last word before the final chorus is "shore." If the last word is, in fact, the lost word, then what has been lost is precisely the ground on which the speaker stands, and he's left adrift at sea. The song doesn't end so much as dissolve, the last note a hollow, barely audible drone.

---

32 Mitchell (2006: p. 69).

"Guiding Light"

If there's a moment of soul-searching on *Marquee Moon*, it comes with dramatic shift in tone that ushers in "Guiding Light," a quietly soulful tune that glimmers through the darkness like a distant lighthouse or an *ignis fatuus*. "Do I, Do I? / belong to the night?" Verlaine opens over chiming piano octaves, metronomic guitars, and Fred Smith's funkiest bass line on this virtually funk-free album. Questioning the entire landscape of the previous five tracks, the song's opening line begs the question of relationship between the "I" and the songwriter, since authorship is doubled here: this is the only track whose words are jointly credited to Verlaine and Lloyd.

Everything on "Guiding Light" — the slower tempo, the delicate guitar work and drums, light bells that chime in the background, the piano part dangling above the chorus — suggests an earnest attempt to escape the urban out-of-doors and retreat — where? Inside, with "all the ladies"? Possibly. The "ladies [who] stay inside" contrast the only other feminine presence on the album thus far: the Venus de Milo, who stands not only for love but for sexual desire, and more importantly who greets the wandering friends in that song out of doors. The contrast between "the night" and a feminized domesticity suggests that the song's title may refer to the soap opera of the same title. The singer is unable to "pull a trick," which may play on "trick" as slang for sex with a prostitute, but may also simply refer to the inability to pull oneself together:

"Never the rose / Without the prick," Verlaine puns. As the song moves toward its final verse, a hush falls and the singer finds himself trapped by time itself: "Time may freeze," he suggests early on, and now "I woke up and it was yesterday." The feeling is cyclical, the movements are unmoored, and only the guiding light of unspecified source is helping to "get thru these nights." As the final verse arrives, the music swells, moving from bass and minimal guitar to a controlled solo that resolves into a repeated line by Lloyd (his eight-layer multi-track ringing like church bells). All of this rides over the layers of a recurring piano line and Ficca's cymbals like the gradual crest of an incoming tide. In the final verse the singer parts from a love "like the seas" parted for Moses, cymbals shimmering like the sound inside a shell. Escape may be possible, in other words, but not for both of them. The sense of victory is muted: is this a triumph over night, or merely *this* night — a note that time has passed after all, that it's not frozen, that it can't repeat itself?

"Prove It"

With "Prove It" the album returns to the realm of Television oldies, a faithful fan favorite since the band first performed it in 1974. Each band member enters "Prove It" separately, sounding a distinct presence. Like "Marquee Moon," this song is essentially a chamber piece: we follow each line separately through the song, getting one of the clearest examples of how intensely this band can focus together, put each part into a perfectly moving whole.

With the exception of "Guiding Light," this is the album's lightest song, opening over a vaguely Latin rhythm that references the Brill Building's golden era, the sound Leiber and Stoller brought to the Drifters and, later, the Shangri-Las, or that Phil Spector created for the Crystals or the Ronettes. Songs like "Uptown" and "Spanish Harlem." The song's closest cousins from other CBGB's bands are "Venus of Avenue D" or "Spanish Stroll" from Mink DeVille, whose Latin-inflected concoction of Sam Cooke and Lou Reed spoke more to Loisaida sounds than most other CB's bands. (Willy DeVille, in his "Venus," sounds like a tough guy sitting on the hood of a Caddy, wearing an alligator-skin jacket, threatening to throw knives at Tom Verlaine's toes.) Of their own output, the closest relation to "Prove It" is Lloyd's solo from "O Mi Amore," or the whole of late takes on "Hard On Love," both of which pick up on the same Latin vibes. Along with Television's "Prove It" and Mink DeVille's "Spanish Stroll," Blondie's girl-group send-up "In the Flesh" or their cover of the Shangri-Las' "Out in the Streets" could have been combined to make a Lower East Side version of *West Side Story* or *Grease*, the latter of which played on Broadway through the entire CB's golden era.

Unlike most of the songs on *Marquee Moon*, the reference points aren't entirely banished here. And it's understandable: the CB's scene was so enamored of the Shangri-Las that Lenny Kaye briefly helped the group reassemble in the mid-'70s for a CB's show and some sessions for Sire that were, unfortunately, never released. Snatched up and thrust into stardom while still high school girls in Queens in the '60s, the Shangri-Las were, ironically, so young during their fleeting fame that they were actually younger than most of the CB's acts who paid them homage a decade later, including Debbie Harry. And yet "Prove It" can't be reduced simply to Brill Building nostalgia or pastiche. There are no castanets, and though the song carries a bit of Ben E. King in its chord progression, by the time Verlaine's first "Prove it!" escapes him, we realize we're on much more tormented ground than you find in "Stand By Me."

Two things become clear if we situate "Prove It" in *Marquee Moon*'s urban night cycle. One, the speaker, in spite of the domesticity invoked in "Guiding Light," has still fallen asleep out of doors, down by the docks. When the song opens it's just before dawn, birds chirping. Waves lap, as do "waves / of light the unreal night," which seems to invoke all the songs we've already heard. The second thing that becomes clear is that the speaker is still hung up on love to the point of derangement. The sense of disorientation persists not only in the high to low soloing, cascading downward scales that suggests a fall (echoes of "Venus"?). Other echoes suggest upward movement: the hundred-foot leap in the second verse recalls the desire to "jumpjumpjump / jump a mountain" in "See No Evil." On one hand, the derangement could be drug-induced — think of the "flat curving / of a room" in the opening verse, a line that Verlaine had formerly followed with: "It gets so funny." The world may just be the projections of a deranged mind — on psychedelics? — losing its "sense of human." But the singer could also be in "in [love] so deep / you could write the Book [of Love]," another favorite figure of '50s pop music. As a parable about falling in love, the song makes a certain amount of sense: hesitation gives way to adventure as "first you creep / then you leap / up about a hundred feet." (Ficca's clever drumroll and cymbal crash, bordering on a rimshot, add emphasis.) Euphoria sets in. Birds feed the singer lines like something out of a Disney film. And "The world is just a feeling / you undertook. / Remember?"

That question calls attention to the song's narrative point of view. It opens as a story about "him" waking up near the docks, though in the second verse the address shifts to second person (you creep / you leap). When the singer asks "Remember?" he could be trying to talk down either himself or a companion. If the former, he could be calling himself to the recognition that his entire consciousness has become wrapped up in this affair. If the latter, he could still be in love. Ego disintegrates; comforts settle in, all warm, calm, and perfect. And the feeling is difficult to describe: it's "too 'too too' / to put a finger on."[33] The sense is less that words fail than that they are superseded by something better.

---

33 Leo Casey made a good case for this reading on the Marquee Moon Mailing List in March 2004.

That sense of indefinite bliss, however, seems at odds with the song's governing refrain, the gumshoe's demand for "just the facts." How can you prove what can't be pinned down? When Richard Hell used Verlaine's line as an epigraph for his pseudo-review of a Television show in 1974, he attributed it both to Sergeant Joe Friday, Jack Webb's character on the '50s TV cop drama *Dragnet*, and to Verlaine in this song. The relationship between Television and hard-boiled noir was something Patti Smith had picked up during Television's first year: she mentions in her *Rock Scene* piece both Phillip Marlow and Jack the Ripper; in the earlier version she had made the claim that Hell's suit had once belonged to Raymond Chandler. From the detective-story standpoint, the song isn't simply an account of falling in love, but also is an investigation of the facts of love, a tougher case to close. Hell, though, wrote "Jest the facts" instead of "just": joke them, in other words. Humorous wordplay evinces a sense of human. Alternating between what could be a rather sweet love song and a chorus that apes a TV detective's interrogation creates a sense of comedy that heightens if we consider that Sergeant Friday's tagline actually comes from a parody of Webb's character by the comedian Stan Freberg, who issued a number of *Dragnet* send-ups on 78 rpm records in the early '50s. The sense of parody is heightened in Verlaine's earliest recorded versions of the song: all the way through the Island demo he camps up the chorus, which, along with the "too 'too too'" line he delivers in his best queeny lisp, mocking social authority. A *Dragnet* drag queen. Let's dress up like cops indeed.

"Torn Curtain"

"Torn Curtain" is the one song fans of this album divide over. It drags. It's melodramatic. It certainly could have been sacrificed in order to make room for other, more popular songs from Television's live set: "Foxhole" or "I Don't Care," both of which would be held over to *Adventure*, or "O Mi Amore," the crowd favorite that would only be released years later as an untitled instrumental on the *Marquee Moon* reissue. And yet there's something thematically appropriate about finishing the album with a funeral dirge.

The song opens with the drumroll from Tony Williams's "Emergency" (1969), a key recording for both Verlaine and Ficca, but instead of kicking into Williams's high-gear, drum-fueled jazz fusion, "Torn Curtain" slows things by half (the opening drum is twice as long, for starters) and moves into chord progressions Verlaine says he borrowed from Stravinsky.[34] Though the drumroll sounds like a prelude, the song serves as the album's epilogue. A case has already been closed at the end of "Prove It." The curtain has come down, that is, before the song starts, and then the curtain's torn, revealing another scene backstage. The song's title invokes the rending of the temple veil in Matthew 27:51, an apocalyptic miracle in the wake of Jesus' crucifixion: "At that moment the curtain of the temple was torn in two from top to bottom. The earth shook and the rocks split." At the same time, the figure

---

34 Licht (2003).

of the curtain points to live rock's theatrical origins. How many rock venues in New York occupy what were once vaudeville theaters?

If a torn curtain lets us see behind the scenes, suggesting vulnerability to exposure, there's a world-weariness to this song that outdoes even the line "I've been working on so long" from the prior track. And the notion that the album ends with a lamentation for wasted "YEARS . . . Flowing by like tears," amid wailing guitars, would seem to underscore the idea that all was not right with the world at the end of "Prove It." If the urban night has been a stage, for the characters on *Marquee Moon* it's one whose devices are left out in the open when the show is over, a stage set. To the degree that the title invokes the Hitchcock film of the same name, we're still in a world of noir. "Burn it down," Verlaine says at the end, a nod to the arson obsession that runs through his poetry and was an integral part of the mythology he'd created with Richard Hell. You get the feeling he's burning evidence.

In a post–*Marquee Moon* interview, Verlaine tells a different story about fire:

> My closest brush with arson came during my first decade when I nearly torched Grover Perdue's back pasture. The field was a haven for havoc, the Edge of the neighborhood, and it was there we prayed an airplane would crash (no such luck). The first, I suppose, was a little private rite between us and the sky to conspiratorialize the afternoon. Unfortunately, the situation quickly got too hot to handle, and though we stamped around the

edges, the circle was expanding faster than we could run around it. Television plays dangerous like this.[35]

And so the album ends with punk's revolutionary injunction: burn it down and start again.

---

35 Demorest (1977).

7
A Record Should Exhaust You by the Time It's Done

Verlaine vacationed in London in February 1977. *Marquee Moon* had come out in the States and he chose to skip town. Since it wouldn't drop in England until March, he was taken off guard to find the band on the cover of *New Musical Express* one morning, complete with the headline: "TELEVISION: Vinyl Masterwork for Spring Schedules Everywhere." Even more surprising: the rave review inside came from Richard Hell's old heroin buddy, Nick Kent:

> Sometimes it takes but one record — one cocksure magical statement — to cold-cock all the crapola and all-purpose wheatchaff mix 'n' match, to set the whole schmear straight and get the current state of play down down down to stand or fall in one, dignified granite-hard focus. Such statements, are precious indeed.[1]

---

1 Kent (1977a).

Two years had passed since Television first received notice from UK music writers who'd ventured to the Bowery looking for the next big thing, and Television had been harder than most to convey in print. (Hell's photos, Kent noted, fared better on the transatlantic voyage.) But here was a record to set things straight at last, one "not fashioned merely for the N.Y. avant-garde rock cognoscenti. It is a record for everyone who boasts a taste for a new exciting music expertly executed, finely in tune, sublimely arranged."[2]

Television's fans had worried that their live electricity wouldn't transfer to vinyl. "Little Johnny Jewel," which received some initial thumbs down, had been a test case in that regard. But reviews for *Marquee Moon* were overwhelmingly positive, with many, like Kent, declaring the album an instant classic. The *Voice's* Robert Christgau placed the album at the top of his 1977 list. It landed at No. 3 on his annual composite "Pazz & Jop" poll of music critics he respected, coming in just behind the Sex Pistols' *Anarchy in the UK* and Elvis Costello's *My Aim Is True* but just ahead of Fleetwood Mac's *Rumours*. The quick take in Christgau's annual consumer's guide was as effusive as Kent's:

> I know why people complain about Tom Verlaine's angst-ridden voice, but fuck that, I haven't had such intense pleasure from a new release since I got into *Layla* three months after it came out, and this took about fifteen seconds. The lyrics, which are in a

2 Kent (1977a).

demotic-philosophical mode ("I was listening/listening to the rain/I was hearing/hearing something else"), would carry this record alone; so would the guitar playing, as lyrical and piercing as Clapton or Garcia but totally unlike either. Yes, you bet it rocks. And no, I didn't believe they'd be able to do it on record because I thought this band's excitement was all in the live raveups. Turns out that's about a third of it.[3]

Christgau's friend Lester Bangs, having given up on Detroit's depleted scene and moved to New York, gave his top honors that year to Richard Hell & the Voidoids, refusing to put Television on his list at all (as did Greil Marcus, who gave the Sex Pistols his top slot).[4] But even Bangs gave begrudging kudos in a review for the glossy mainstream rock weekly, *Circus*, though he couldn't resist slamming the band for being just plain boring as people: "The grooves of Television's first album are the most interesting of the year so far," he wrote. "The group has been compared to the Velvet Underground and the Stooges, and I thought citifried Grateful Dead when I saw them live, but none of that really holds re this LP." He concluded by repeating the confession that he likes the album in spite of himself: "it's not pretentious, it has a gritty churn that'll get in your blood like specks of gravel or the rust that comes to neon." It wouldn't sell, he predicted, because it doesn't sound like the corporate hard rockers Boston, but that's half the reason he likes it: "So thrash on

---

3 Christgau (1991: p. 391).
4 Christgau (1978a).

and bless you, Verlaine," he ends, revealing just how personal this review has been, "even if you are a creep and never think about jumping a little bit on stage like this guy Richard Hell in the news? Now there's an image of a rock 'n' roll prince, later for stars (that's for you, Patti)."[5]

Christgau noted that his year-end poll indexed an industry watershed: the top three artists were all "rank amateurs." (He doesn't say "punks," but all three fell under that loose umbrella as well.) In retrospect other signs are visible: what Christgau had famously dubbed the "Rock-Critic Establishment" had thrown its weight, in 1977, behind UK rather than New York punk. The "punk" label would haunt Television in multiple ways, leading Verlaine to think for years that it, along with too close an identification with the New York scene, had stymied Television's commercial breakthrough. Following a cross-country American tour in spring 1977 (incongruously supporting Peter Gabriel, a fan of the band but most popular among prog rockers who detested punk) the band spent most of May and June touring the UK and Europe to audiences eager to see the group that had long been lionized as punk founders. The mythology of CBGB's, partially their creation, preceded them. With mainstream media already equating "punk" with the fashion sensibility McLaren and the Sex Pistols had popularized — already three-years old in New York have having lost a little of its edge — Television puzzled reviewers and some audience members who expected flashier stage antics or the snottiness and violence associated with UK punks. Television, by contrast, seemed "cold," an assessment buttressed by press accounts, hardly exaggerated, of icy relations with their supporting act, Blondie. The album, which sold much better in the UK than it did at home, peaked on the British charts at No. 28.

Back home in February, amid encouraging early reviews and not yet on the road to support the album, the band played three triumphal nights at CBGB's. John Rockwell, in the *Times*, warned, as he had when Patti Smith first signed with Arista, that audiences should hurry downtown, since the group couldn't play small venues for long. "There's a certain point where you think you deserve something," Verlaine told Rockwell. The article ran with a large close-up of the singer glancing to the side of the frame, cigarette ash aglow. "I'm sick of playing places where we bump into things." This was a comment Verlaine made more than once that spring. When Rockwell rattles off the now familiar story of how Television stumbled onto CBGB's three years earlier, Verlaine comments with confidence on his role in the interaction with Kristal: "I went and asked him, 'Why don't you play rock here?' . . . He wasn't making any money so he said, 'Why not?' Soon we got a following, and every band in the world converged on the place."[6]

True to Rockwell's prediction, Television never played CBGB's again, a clear signal of Verlaine's

---

6 Rockwell (1977b).

increased distance from the scene. Many assumed he had shrugged it off in direct mimicry of Dylan reject- ing the folk movement, as if he and Patti Smith had conspired to imitate jointly Dylan's cool detachment on display in *Don't Look Back*.[7]

On returning from their European tour, the band headlined a few dates in the Midwest, then returned to New York, though they dropped out of sight on the local scene, especially Verlaine. One reason was purely financial: with no money to show for their troubles, they sold off their equipment to live. Over a decade later Verlaine insisted they had never made royalties on the album beyond the initial advance. Other troubled plagued them: Lloyd had parlayed the band's critical cache, and a mutual rehab doctor, into a friendship with Anita Pallenberg, Keith Richards's girlfriend. Their shared habit led them into adventures such as roaming the Lower East Side in a limo, looking for their dealer. ("The dealers were like, 'GET THAT FUCKING LIMO OFF MY BLOCK! WHAT ARE YOU, CRAZY?" he recalled in *Please Kill Me*.[8]) Lloyd's addiction ominously echoed the one that had been partly responsible for alienating Verlaine from Hell two years earlier.

Still, the band threw its energy into recording a follow-up record, *Adventure*. That album — which had a cleaner sound and poppier production than the debut, tracks like "Days" and "Glory" in retrospect seeming

---

7 Bangs (1977); Cf. McNeil and McCain (1996: pp. 195–6).
8 McNeil and McCain (1996: pp. 303).

to predict a decade of American college rock — fared well with American critics generally but received mixed reactions on the local scene and in the UK. Roy Trakin, reviewing the album for *New York Rocker* (which was generally supportive of Television), predicted that "die-hard Television addicts are gonna be disappointed with this LP" and thought it "eliminates much of the fiery dynamism the band still manages in live performance."[9] Trakin's criticism was rooted in the album's recording history: Richard Lloyd had spent several weeks in the hospital in the middle of the recording sessions with a heart inflammation, endocarditis, brought on, as he acknowledged, by shooting up. As a result his presence on the album is severely diminished. The same issue of *New York Rocker* featured Television as one of New York's top 10 bands, but gave them only 7–1 odds of breaking into the mainstream: "Their followup has insiders buzzing, but the group's low public profile hurts their immediate chances for widespread expo-sure. Ultimately it must be in the grooves and if FM programmers ever wake up to the fact, they'll find that Television possesses strong 'crossover' potential."[10] Many on the scene seemed to take Television's "low public profile" personally.

If such withdrawal had hurt them at home, the enthu-siasm they had generated in the UK quickly spawned a backlash. The *NME*'s Julie Burchill, nursing grudges against her rival writer Nick Kent, savaged *Adventure*

---

9 Trakin (1978).
10 "N.Y. Bands" (1978).

and the whole New York scene, under the headline "The TV Backlash Starts Here." Kent's endorsement of *Marquee Moon*, she suggested, had prompted that album's unwarranted success by "auto-suggest[ion]." In her view, Verlaine's "acid-casualty-type-gibberish" lyrics were sufficient only for him and Patti Smith to curl up and read French poetry to. Though not all critics agreed by any means, a backlash — perhaps inevitable, considering years of hype — did seem in the works. A British tour in support of the album drew crowds, the album outsold *Marquee Moon* (making it to No. 7 on the UK charts), but even supportive critics fretted enthusiasm for the band had declined.

By the late summer of '77 it seemed apparent that the new wave of British punk bands would define the movement that had been lumped under that umbrella term. Alan Betrock, in *New York Rocker*, sounded slightly resentful: "What the Ramones, Blondie, Patti, and Television started well over two years ago has now become the biggest force in rock 'n' roll," he wrote. "Only one suspects that the English new-wave, with their more extreme politics, sounds, and costumes . . . will bear the fruits of New York's labor."[11] The Sex Pistols, writer Lisa Jane Persky complained in the same issue, were nothing more than a Monster made up of bits McLaren stole from early Television and the Ramones. If the band was hampered by transatlantic expectations of what "punk" meant, at home Verlaine felt they had been pigeonholed as a New York band,

---

11 Betrock (1977).

which made it difficult to get mainstream airplay. To make matters worse, Elektra was not supporting the band domestically, instead favoring the London market, which had shown more initial interest. For years Verlaine would complain that the label had chosen to throw its weight behind Bostonian newcomers the Cars — a band with a similar sound but a softer, more pleasant vocals and glossier, radio-friendly production. (The Cars, he said, had broken through by relying on "automatic reference points," exactly what he had hoped to avoid in his own work.[12]) In *Marquee Moon*'s wake, Verlaine had told the Boston *Phoenix* that there's "so much prejudice against New Yorkers it's incredible. In a town like St. Louis, you can't even get played on the radio if you're from New York. You walk into a radio station and the guy looks at you like, 'Here's another bunch of New York assholes.' It makes you either want to be an asshole or try to get through to the guy. I don't mind if they play the record or not, but I'd really like it if they'd listen to it. We're a different sort of band from what they're used to, so I think we're worth a listen." A year later, following *Adventure*'s release, he echoed the complaint to Richard Robinson in *Hit Parader*:

> If people still think we are a punk rock band, they're not even going to listen to this record. I mean I know, especially among radio people, I know how they are — "Oh another New York punk band" phhhewwt they're

---

12 Kozak (1981).

not even going to open it. If people listen to, you know, Fleetwood Mac — they're going to think our first record was grating. There's all guitars, no sweet harmonies, I mean sure. They're just going to hear it as like exhausting or something. I mean I like that about our records. I think a record should exhaust you by the time it's done, otherwise it's not even worth the seven dollars.[13]

When the band did play New York again — three nights at the Bottom Line in July 1978 — they were homecoming shows in multiple senses. The band hadn't played the city for 18 months, and they'd just returned from a UK tour and several successful West Coast shows. Christgau, in an enthusiastic review, highlighted the gulf that separated the band from their erstwhile scenemates:

Television's disappearance from Manhattan music over the past year and a half has emphasized their musical distance from the flourishing little club scene they helped create. For although they started out post-Velvets, and although "Blank Generation," which now passes for an anthem at CBGB, began life as a showpiece for Television's first bassist, Richard Hell, the term punk sits even more oddly on this band than on Talking Heads. At least the Heads remain committed to their own versions of two basic punk principles, brevity and manic intensity, but Television's principles, as both admirers and detractors have observed, are throwbacks to the psychedelic era. These musicians are lyrical, spaced out, and obscure, and they don't live in fear of boring

---

13 Robinson (1978).

somebody. Never mind the raveups and long solos —
many of their *intros*, in which single riffs repeat again
and again, stretch toward the one-minute mark, about
where the Ramones begin the chorus.[14]

Christgau concluded by pin-pointing the band's
iconoclastic Utopianism, derived from its bohemian
heritage, as its defining feature. They were a revolution
unto themselves, a self-contained vanguard unwilling to
be associated with the train that followed: "Television is
representative of nothing," Christgau wrote. "Almost
every great rock band and a lot of the most successful
bad ones culminate some general social tendency,
be it the Ramones' pop economy or Kansas's greedy
middle-American pseudo-seriousness or Steely Dan's
expert programmability or Kiss's life-sized caricature.
But while it's possible to imagine a late-'60s revival in
which Television would spawn countless imitators, at
the moment their single-minded Utopian individual-
ism sets them apart. And it is just that that makes them
seem so precious."[15]

What Christgau couldn't have known is that within
two months the band would throw in the towel.

When that announcement came in September,
Television's breakup heralded, for many, the end of
an era. Alan Betrock printed an obituary for the band
in *New York Rocker*, along with a two-page spread
that featured photos of the band's final shows and a

---

14 Christgau (1978b).
15 Christgau (1978b).

full-page reproduction of the homemade flier for a Max's show with Patti Smith four years earlier. The breakup made Betrock fret for the life of underground rock in general. As the title of another piece in the same issue asked, was this "New Wave Goodbye?" Betrock's postmortem is deeply personal, revealing how closely critics as well as musicians had pinned their own stories to this scene, which helps to explain the enduring appeal of the CBGB's mythology: if other bands would successfully break into the mainstream, Television would be the band that remained so true to its principles that they doomed themselves to an early death and cult status. Automatic authenticity.

"SO TELEVISION has broken up and most people want to know why," Betrock began:

> There must be a story there: find out who did what, who said such and such, how much each record sold, and so on. But all that behind-the-scenes stuff is totally beside the point. Does it really matter why? I mean, are there lessons to be learned, mistakes to be circumvented, follies to be unearthed? I think not. Out of New York, they played bars still, college towns with half-filled houses, on stages more accustomed to local amateurs than visionary professionals. Chris Stamey [of the dB's] said: "They were my favorite band. It's probably the last time I'll ever have a favorite." And he was right.
>
> There were off nights. Granted. There were weak spots. Granted. There were tactical errors, production deficiencies, and hurt egos. All granted. But there was brilliance. There were times when the roof would fly away and we sailed upwards like UFO's on the Bowery.

Perhaps there was just too much to be contained in one unit.

. . . Now perhaps you wonder if this isn't all a little too serious. Like, I mean, "Hey, all right already, a great rock band broke up. But there'll be new ones and spinoffs and solo albums, and commercial success and more great music. So c'mon, what's the big deal?"

Well, I dunno really. But something is gone, something is lost forever. Something that leaves you feeling a little more alone, a little more empty, and a little more helpless. It gets you in the gut, in the pit of your stomach, where it seems to churn and warn you in advance that something painful is on the horizon. They are survived by artifacts, plastic and mercurial, photos and snapshots of an era that went by too fast and will never come again. They are faded now, unfocussed, unsmiling and cold. I'm feeling kind of cold now myself. Kind of distant. Kind of mixed up and drifting. A beacon has vanished. The anchor is gone. TV is dead. Long live TV.[16]

---

16 Betrock (1978).

Coda

> Village lore had it that whenever you spotted [Tom] Verlaine in daylight, it was a good omen.
> — *James Wolcott*, The Catsitters: A Novel *(2009)*

Over the next dozen years, Verlaine released half a dozen solo records, some of which sold better than Television's albums initially had, all of which deserve larger audiences than they've enjoyed, but none of which made him a household name. *Marquee Moon*, like *The Velvet Underground and Nico*, enjoyed wider acclaim from subsequent generations of musicians and critics than it did from general audiences. *Rolling Stone* lists it as number 128 on its list of all-time greatest rock albums; in 2003 the *NME* ranked it much higher, at number four, beating out anything by the Beatles, the Stones, or Bob Dylan. I was a teenager in the '80s, and though I lived in the Arizona sticks, I knew enough from reading *Rolling Stone* and *Spin* that the post-punk bands soundtracking my smalltown angst — REM, U2,

Echo and the Bunnymen, the Smiths, the Cure — all cited Television and other CB's bands as primary influences. Still, as a teenager I didn't know anyone who owned *Marquee Moon*, let alone Verlaine's solo stuff. When, in my early twenties, I finally found Television's albums and bootlegs, they were both familiar and disorienting on first listen, the way you might feel when you find an ancestor's photograph in an attic trunk and see some of yourself in that strange face.

Richard Lloyd's three solo albums through the mid-'80s tended toward bluesy riffs, and though his licks continued to be highly regarded, he didn't quite carry Verlaine's following. In the late '80s and early '90s he performed with power popster Matthew Sweet, an avowed Television fan. Fred Smith played on both Lloyd's and Verlaine's solo records. Billy Ficca drummed for the new wave band The Waitresses and rejoined Verlaine in 1992 for his seventh solo release. That same year Television reunited as well, releasing a third album that, though it contained solid songs and was well received critically, didn't reach the heights of their original incarnation and couldn't possibly live up to the legendary status and influence the first two records had attained. The band played festival dates in the wake of the reunion record, then took another hiatus, this one eight years long, before returning to the festival circuit at 2001's All Tomorrow's Parties. Over the next half dozen years the band made occasional appearances. In 2004 they played shows in New York with Patti Smith to mark the 30th anniversary of their first co-headline at Max's. They even toyed with recording another album before Lloyd left the band for good in 2007, replaced by guitarist Jimmy Rip, who had long supported Verlaine's solo recordings and live sets.

When CBGB's closed in the fall of 2006 — Hilly Kristal unable or unwilling to renegotiate his lease and the back-rent he owed the non-profit Bowery Residents' Coalition — New York's media outlets and many fans mourned, even those who hadn't been into the club in decades. Television received requisite nods as founders in most accounts of the club's history, though unlike other early CB's performers — David Byrne, Patti Smith — Verlaine kept his distance from the closing drama. Hilly planned to take the club to Las Vegas, even the urinals, but instead his 2007 death left his family scrapping with one another over inheritance and the club's lucrative trademark logo.

Patti Smith headlined the club's final shows. Standing out front, amidst crowds, reporters, and paparazzi, she snapped her own photo of the famous awning. "I'm sentimental," she told the *Times*, blaming the closing on "the new prosperity of our city." She encouraged kids to go somewhere else — anywhere — to start scenes of their own: "CBGB's is a state of mind."[1] As part of her three-hour final set, which would culminate in her reading the names of CBGB's dead over the last strains of her song "Elegie," Smith performed songs that invoked her history with the space, including "We Three," which she'd originally

---

1 Sisario (2006).

written about her, Verlaine, and Lanier, and which refers to the club in the opening lines. She read the lyrics to "Marquee Moon" with Lloyd backing her on guitar. Recalling her first Television show in April 1974, she saluted the band for its role in establishing the scene. She'd been recording new music with Tom Verlaine the night before, she said, then added with a smile that "he reluctantly sends his love."

Bibliography

Manuscript Holdings

Richard Hell Papers, Fales Library and Special Collections, New York University.

Web Sites

CBGB & OMFUG http://cbgb.com/
It's All the Streets You Crossed Not So Long Ago http://streetsyoucrossed.blogspot.com/
Marc Miller's 98 Bowery http://98bowery.com/
Richard Hell http://richardhell.com/
Richard Lloyd http://richardlloyd.com/
Rock's Back Pages http://rocksbackpages.com/
This Ain't the Summer of Love http://thisaintthesummeroflove.blogspot.com/
The Wonder http://www.thewonder.co.uk/

Online Publications

Bangs, Lester. "Who Are the Real Dictators?" unpublished, March 1976, posted at http://punkmagazine.com in 2000.

Now available at http://www.jimdero.com/Bangs/Bangs%20
Punk.htm

Dalton, David. "What Fresh Hell Is This?" *Gadfly Online*, 19
November 2001. http://www.gadflyonline.com/11-19-01/
book-richardhell.html

"Endurance: The Richard Lloyd Interview," *Rock Town Hall*,
16 May 2007. http://www.rocktownhall.com/blogs/index.
php/endurance_the_richard_lloyd_interview

Fritscher, Jack. "Introduction" to "The Academy:
Incarceration for Pleasure," *The Best of Drummer Magazine*,
at www.JackFritscher.com

Gross, Jason. "Richard Hell Interview." *Perfect Sound
Forever*, December 1997. http://www.furious.com/perfect/
richardhell.html

Hell, Richard. "Favorite Music." *Perfect Sound Forever*, 1997.
http://www.furious.com/perfect/staff2.html#richardhell

Hoffmann, Kristian. Mumps History. http://www.
kristianhoffman.com/mumps-history.htm

Kristal, Hilly, "The History of CBGB & OMFUG." http://
www.cbgb.com/history1.htm

Kugel, Barry, Interview with Tom Verlaine, originally in *Big
Star*, May 1977, available online at http://ffanzeen.blogspot.
com/2010/06/talkin-with-televisions-tom-verlaine-at.html
(Posted in June 2010)

Lloyd, Richard. "Ask Richard." http://www.richardlloyd.com/
solute.htm

— email to Leo Casey, 20 October 2007, posted to Marquee
Moon Discussion List on 22 October 2007.

Rader, Jim. "Close-Up: A Fan's Notes on the Early Years,"
Perfect Sound Forever, February 2009. http://www.furious.
com/perfect/televisionearly.html

"Richard Lloyd, Man on the Marquee Moon," *Rock Town Hall*,
20 April 2009. http://www.rocktownhall.com/blogs/index.
php/richard-lloyd-man-on/

Swirsky, Bryan. "Richard Hell — Exclusive Interview,"

TrakMarx, 12 (December 2003). http://www.trakmarx.com/2003_05/

Veillette, Eric. "Perfect Sound Forever online magazine presents Richard Lloyd" *Perfect Sound Forever*, November 2000. http://www.furious.com/perfect/richardlloyd.html

Books

Banes, Sally. *Greenwich Village 1963* (Durham: Duke UP, 1993).

Bangs, Lester. *Blondie* (New York: Fireside,1980).

—*Psychotic Reactions and Carburetor Dung* (New York: Vintage Books, 1988).

Bayley, Roberta, Stephanie Chernikowski, George du Bose, Godlis, Bob Gruen, and Ebet Roberts, *Blank Generation Revisited: The Early Days of Punk Rock* (New York: Schirmer,1997).

Bockris, Victor and Roberta Bayley. *Patti Smith: An Unauthorized Biography* (New York: Simon and Schuster, 1999).

— and Gerard Malanga. *Up-Tight: The Velvet Underground Story* (London: Omnibus,1983).

Cagle, Van M. *Reconstructing Pop/Subculture: Art, Rock, and Andy Warhol* (Thousand Oaks, CA: Sage,1995).

Christgau, Robert. *Rock Albums of the '70s* (New York: Da Capo, 1991).

Chrome, Cheetah. *Cheetah Chrome: A Dead Boy's Tale: From the Front Lines of Punk Rock* (Minneapolis: Voyageur, 2010).

County, Jayne. *Man Enough to Be a Woman* (London: Serpent's Tail,1995).

DeLillo, Don. *Great Jones Street* (Boston: Houghton Mifflin, 1973).

DeRogatis, Jim. *Let It Blurt: The Life & Times of Lester Bangs* (New York: 2000).

—*The Velvet Underground: An Illustrated History of a Walk on the Wild Side* (Minneapolis: Voyageur, 2009).

Fletcher, Tony. *All Hopped Up and Ready to Go: Music from the Streets of New York, 1927–77* (New York: W.W. Norton, 2009).

Gavin, James. *Intimate Nights: The Golden Age of New York Cabaret* (New York: Back Stage, 2006).

Gendron, Bernard. *Between Montmarte and the Mudd Club: Popular Music and the Avant-Garde* (Chicago: University of Chicago Press, 2002).

Gimarc, George. *Punk Diary: The Ultimate Trainspotter's Guide to Underground Rock, 1970–1982* (San Francisco: Backbeat, 2005).

Goldberg, Danny. *Bumping into Geniuses: My Life inside the Rock and Roll Business* (New York: Gotham, 2008).

Gorman, Paul. *In Their Own Write: Adventures in the Music Press* (London: Sanctuary, 2001).

Gray, Timothy. *Urban Pastoral: Natural Currents in the New York School* (Iowa City: University of Iowa Press, 2010).

Grunenberg, Christoph, and Jonathan Harris, *Summer of Love: Psychedelic Art, Social Crisis, and Counterculture in the 1960s* (Liverpool: Liverpool University Press, 2005).

Harry, Debbie, Chris Stein, and Victor Bockris, *Making Tracks: The Rise of Blondie* (New York: Da Capo, 1998 [1982]).

Hell, Richard. *Hot and Cold* (New York: powerHouse, 2001).

—*The Voidoid* (Hove, UK: Codex, 1996).

Heylin, Clinton. *Babylon's Burning: From Punk to Grunge* (New York: Canongate, 2007).

—*From the Velvets to the Voidoids: A Pre-Punk History for a Post-Punk World* (Chicago: Chicago Review, 1993).

Kane, Daniel. *All Poets Welcome: The Lower East Side Poetry Scene in the 1960s* (Berkeley: University of California Press, 2003).

Kent, Nick. *Apathy for the Devil: A Seventies Memoir* (New York: Faber & Faber, 2010).

Killen, Andreas. *1973 Nervous Breakdown: Watergate, Warhol, and the Birth of Post-Sixties America* (New York: Bloomsbury USA, 2006).

Kozak, Roman. *This Ain't No Disco: The Story of CBGB* (Boston: Faber & Faber, 1988).

Lawrence, Tim. *Hold On to Your Dreams: Arthur Russell and the Downtown Music Scene, 1973–1992* (Durham: Duke University Press, 2009).

Leigh, Mickey, with Legs McNeil. *I Slept with Joey Ramone* (New York: Touchstone, 2009).

Marcus, Greil. *Like a Rolling Stone: Bob Dylan at the Crossroads* (New York: PublicAffairs, 2005).

McNeil, Legs, and Gillian McCain. *Please Kill Me: The Uncensored Oral History of Punk* (New York: Grove, 1996).

Mele, Christopher. *Selling the Lower East Side: Culture, Real Estate, and Resistance in New York City* (Minneapolis: University of Minnesota Press, 2000).

Meltzer, Richard. *A Whore Just Like the Rest* (New York: Da Capo, 2000).

Mitchell, Tim. *Sonic Transmission: Television, Tom Verlaine, Richard Hell* (London: Glitter, 2006). Chapter 12 is missing from the print volume but is available at http://www.timmitchell.org.uk/Sonic%202.html

Nobakht, David. *Suicide: No Compromise* (London: SAF, 2005).

Patell, Cyrus R. K. and Bryan Waterman, eds. *The Cambridge Companion to the Literature of New York* (New York: Cambridge University Press, 2010).

—*Lost New York, 1609–2009* (New York: Fales Library, 2009).

Ramone, Dee Dee, *Lobotomy: Surviving the Ramones* (New York: Da Capo, 2000).

Rombes, Nicholas. *A Cultural Dictionary of Punk, 1974–1982* (New York: Continuum, 2009).

—*Ramones* (New York: Continuum, 2005).

Sarig, Roni. *The Secret History of Rock* (New York: Billboard, 1998).

Savage, Jon. *The* England's Dreaming *Tapes* (Minneapolis: University of Minnesota Press, 2010).

Shelton, Robert. *No Direction Home: The Life and Music of Bob Dylan* (New York: Hal Leonard, 1986).

Smith, Patti. *Just Kids* (New York: Ecco, 2010).

Valentine, Gary. *New York Rocker* (New York: Da Capo, 2006 [2002]).

Zukin, Sharon. *Loft Living: Culture and Capital in Urban Change* (Baltimore: Johns Hopkins University Press, 1982).

Articles, Chapters, and Reviews

"Androgyny in Rock: A Short Introduction," *Creem*, August 1973.

Baker, Robb. "The Honkies and the Gay Menace," *SoHo Weekly News*, 29 May 1975.

—"Off Off and Away," *After Dark*, September 1974.

Bangs, Lester. "Lou Reed: A Deaf Mute in a Telephone Booth," *Let It Rock*, November 1973.

—"Marquee Moon — Television (Elektra)," *Circus*, 14 April 1977.

—"Patti Smith: Horses," *Creem*, February 1976.

Bell, Max. "Tom Foolery: Tom Verlaine," *The Face*, July 1984.

Betrock, Alan. "Good-bye Liverpool, Hello Oblivion?" *SoHo Weekly News*, 22 May 1975a.

—"Know Your New York Bands: Television," *SoHo Weekly News*, 3 April 1975b.

—"New Wave Hangs Ten," *New York Rocker*, July/August 1977.

—"Television at CBGB," *SoHo Weekly News*, 23 January 1975c.

—"Television 1974–1978," *New York Rocker*, September 1978.

Black, Bill. "The Ramones," *Sounds*, 12 January 1985.

"Bowie Knife," *The Advocate*, 14 November 1995: 107.

Bradshaw, Melissa. "Performing Greenwich Village Bohemianism," in Patell and Waterman (eds.), *The Cambridge Companion to the Literature of New York* (New York: Cambridge University Press, 2010), 146–159.

Buckley, Tom. "New Supper Club in Greenwich Village Swims against the Tide," *New York Times*, 23 February 1973.

Charlesworth, Chris. "Blue Oyster Cult: Cult Heroes," *Melody Maker*, 16 February 1974.

—"CBGBs, Max's etc.: Underground Overground," *Melody Maker*, 27 November 1976.

Christgau, Robert. "Avant-Punk: A Cult Explodes . . . and a Movement Is Born," *Village Voice*, 24 October 1977.

—"Bette Midler: The Art of Compassion," *Newsday*, August 1972.

—"Pazz & Joppers Dig Pistols — What Else Is New?" *Village Voice*, 23 January 1978a.

—"Television Don't Play by Numbers," *Village Voice*, 22 March 1976.

—"Television's Principles," *Village Voice*, 19 June 1978b.

Demorest, Stephen. "Another Television Broadside: Tom Verlaine: Genius in Fragments," *Sounds*, 8 April 1978.

—"Television: More Than Just a Boob Tube," *Creem*, May 1977.

Dery, Mark. "The 6 String Alchemy of Richard Lloyd," *Guitar Player*, January 1988.

Dove, Ian. "On the Trail of a New York Sound," *Billboard*, 14 December 1974.

Elliott, George. "TV: Cool Reception," *Crawdaddy!*, January 1977.

Emerson, Ken. "Television Takes to the Air," *Village Voice*, 14 March 1977.

Feigenbaum, Josh. "R&R&B&CW," *SoHo Weekly News*, 25 April 1974.

Fields, Danny. "Interview with Mickey Ruskin," *Andy Warhol's Interview*, April 1973.

—"The *SoHo Weekly News* Columns: Punk's First Press," in Scott Schinder (ed.) *Rolling Stone's Alt-Rock-a-Rama* (New York: Delta, 1996).

Fricke, David, "Interview with Patti Smith (1996)," in Jann Wenner (ed.) *The Rolling Stone Interviews* (New York: Back Bay, 2007).

Gerstenzang, Peter. "Hendrix on His Mind," *New York Times*, 27 February 2009.

Gholson, Craig. "Richard Lloyd: Life, Love, and Electra/Asylum [sic]," *New York Rocker*, September 1976.

Goldman, Vivian. "To Hell & Back," *Sounds*, 8 October 1977.

Green, Penny. "I No Longer Need People to Cloak Me [Patti Smith interview]," *Andy Warhol's Interview*, October 1973.

Harron, Mary. "Pop Art/Art Pop: The Warhol Connection," *Melody Maker*, 16 February 1980.

Hastead, Nick. "Punk's Founding Father: Richard Hell," *The Independent* [London], 19 August 2005.

Hell, Richard. "The Autobiography of Richard Hell," *Brooklyn Rail*, October 2007.

—"I Is Another," *New York Times* [Sunday Book Review], 15 October 2008.

—"'I Was Robbed!' Or, How I Invented Punk Rock," *NME*, 4 May 1980.

—"My First Television Set (1974)," in *Hot and Cold* (New York: powerHouse, 2001), 39–40.

Hermes, Will. "Punk Reunion New York," *Spin*, October 2007: 83–4.

Hibbert, Tom. "The Bowery Beat: CBGBs and All That," *The History of Rock*, 1982.

Hickey, Dave. "Martin on Ramones: Now That's Freedom," *Village Voice*, 21 February 1977.

—"Prime Time: Television," *The History of Rock*, 1983.

—"Television: One Big Happy Family . . .," *Q*, October 1992.

Holmstrom, John. "Jayne County: 'CBGBs was a bit scary!'" *Punk*, Fall 2007.

Jones, Allan. "Television," *Melody Maker*, 18 June 1977.

Joseph, Branden. "'My Mind Split Open': Andy Warhol's Exploding Plastic Inevitable," *Grey Room* (summer 2002): 80–107.

Kane, Daniel, "From Poetry to Punk in the East Village," in Patell and Waterman (eds.), *The Cambridge Companion to the Literature of New York* (New York: Cambridge University Press, 2010), 189–201.

Kaprow, Allan. "'Happenings' in the New York Scene," *Art News* 60:3 (May 1961): 36–9, 58–62.

Kendall, Paul. "Four Guys with a Passion," *ZigZag*, June 1977.

Kent, Nick. "Blue Oyster Cult/Black Oak Arkansas," *NME*, 2 March 1974a.

—"Eno: Of Launderettes and Lizard Girls," *NME*, 28 July 1973a.

—"New York Dolls: Dead End Kids On The Champs-Elysées," *NME*, January 1974b.

—"New York: The Dark Side of the Town," *NME*, 5 May 1973b.

—"Television: Marquee Moon," *NME*, 5 February 1977a.

—"Tom Verlaine: How Pleasant (?) To Know Mr Verlaine," *NME*, 26 March 1977b.

—"A Walk on the Wild Side of Lou Reed," *NME*, 9 June 1973c.

Kozak, Roman. "Verlaine's New Method," *Billboard*, 19 September 1981.

Krauss, Rosalind. "The Originality of the Avant-Garde," *October* (autumn 1981): 47–66.

Laughner, Peter. "Sleeper of the Month," *Creem*, February 1976.

—"Television Proves It," *Creem*, May 1977.

Leichtling, Jerry. "Buddy Holly, Can You Spare a Dime?" *Village Voice*, 14 July 1975.

Licht, Alan. Liner notes. *Marquee Moon* (reissue), Elektra/Rhino, 2003.

—"Out of the Cool," *Wire*, April 2006.

McCormack, Ed. "The Gold Lamé Dream of Bette Midler," *Rolling Stone*, 15 February 1973.

Melillo, John. "Secret Locations in the Lower East Side: Downtown Poetics, 1960–1980," in Patell and Waterman (eds.) *Lost New York, 1609–2009* (New York: Fales Library, 2009), 59–72.

Mengaziol, Peter. "Tom Verlaine Plays with the Focus," *Guitar World*, November 1981.

Miles, "Just Another Tough 'n' Tender Street Poet Outta New Yawk," *NME*, 13 August 1977.

—"New York Dolled Up: Glittermania in Gotham," *International Times*, 1972.

Mortifoglio, Richard. "Watch Television," *Village Voice*, 7 July 1975.

Murray, Charles Shaar. "Down in the Scuzz with the Heavy Cult Figures," *NME*, 7 June 1975a.

—"Hilly Kristal (CBGBs)," *NME*, 4 March 1978.

—"New York: The Sound of '75," *NME*, 8 November 1975b.

Noland, Carrie Jaurès. "Rimbaud and Patti Smith: Style as Social Deviance," *Critical Inquiry* (spring 1995): 581–610.

"N.Y. Bands '78: The Big Ten," *New York Rocker*, February/March 1978.

"*Punk* Talks with Tom Verlaine and Richard Lloyd of Television," *Punk*, March 1976.

Robbins, Ira. "Television," *Mojo*, February 2001.

Robinson, Lisa. "Interview with Tom Verlaine," *Hit Parader*, July 1977.

—"Rebel Nights," *Vanity Fair*, November 2002.

Robinson, Richard. "TV Is on Again," *Hit Parader*, September 1978.

Rockwell, John. "CBGB Club Is Hub for Bands Playing Underground Rock," *New York Times*, 24 January 1976a.

—"Disbanding of the Dolls Tells a Tale of One City," *New York Times*, 25 April 1975a.

—"Imagery by Patti Smith, Poet Turned Performer," *New York Times*, 12 July 1974.

—"John Cale Has Debut at CBGB," *New York Times*, 21 December 1976b.

—"Patti Smith Plans Album With Eyes on Stardom," *New York Times*, 28 March 1975b.

—"The Pop Life," 2 July 1976c.

—"Report from New York's Rock Underground," *New York Times*, 20 February 1977a.

—"Where to Plug Into Television," *New York Times*, 25 February 1977b.

Rose, Frank. "An Elegant Enigma," *The Boston Phoenix*, October 1977.

Sisario, Ben. "CBGB Brings Down the Curtain with Nostalgia and One Last Night of Rock," *New York Times*, 16 October 2006.

Smith, Patti. "Somewhere Somebody Must Stand Naked," *Rock Scene*, October 1974a.

—"Television: Escapees from Heaven," *SoHo Weekly News*, 27 June 1974b.

Strick, Wesley. "Symbolist Coffee Break: A Dream Date With T.V." *The Music Gig*, September 1976.

"Television," *Andy Warhol's Interview*, January 1975.

"Television," *New York Rocker*, March 1977.

"Tom Verlaine," *Musician*, June 1995.

Trakin, Roy. "Soul on Ice," *New York Rocker*, February/March 1978.

—"Tom Verlaine without TV: The New Season," *New York Rocker*, September 1979.

Verlaine, Tom. "Tom Verlaine," *New York Rocker*, February 1976.

Wadsley, Pat. "Guide to the New York Bands." *SoHo Weekly News*, 25 March 1976.

Wildsmith, Steve. "Richard Lloyd Reminisces about His Time with Jimi Hendrix and Television," *Daily Times* (Blount County, TN), 15 October 2009.

Williams, Richard, "It's a Shame That Nobody Listens," *Melody Maker*, 25 October 1969, in Clinton Heylin (ed.) *All Yesterdays' Parties: The Velvet Underground in Print, 1966–1971* (New York: Da Capo, 2005): pp. 119–21.

Wolcott, James. "The Bollocks," *New Yorker*, 22 July 1996.

—"A Conservative Impulse in the New Rock Underground," *Village Voice*, 18 August 1975a.

—"The Rise of Punk Rock," *Village Voice*, 1 March 1976.

—"A Smoking 45," *Village Voice*, 27 October 1975b.

—"Television Is Watching You," *Hit Parader*, March 1977.

Young, Charles M. "Television: Don't Touch That Dial," *Rolling Stone*, 21 April 1977.

Also available in the series